Do You Remember
When You Were Thirteen?

Nicki came to Sunday school with glitter in her hair. Mike swaggered in with the haircut his mother begged him not to get. Jaysen sat in a corner proudly belching. Jessica burst through the door and ran to tug on Gary's sleeve. Her latest life-or-death crisis was that she saw one of her friends smoking in the school's restroom. What were we going to do about it?

Parents and youth workers, don't despair. These children have not developed a sudden case of insanity; they are simply going through a stage. Like temper tantrums and teething, this too will pass.

But what do you do in the meantime?

Discover with Gary and Angela Hunt the keys to surviving the often outlandish, always confusing "tweenage" years. You'll find that life with a tween is not only survivable, but, at times, actually enjoyable.

SURVIVING YOUR CHILD'S MIDDLE SCHOOL YEARS

Too Young to Drive, Too Old to Ride

GARY & ANGELA HUNT

649.1 FM
HUN

First Printing, August 1992

Previously published as *Surviving the Tweenage Years* (San Bernardino, CA: Here's Life Publishers, 1988).

Published by
HERE'S LIFE PUBLISHERS, INC.
P. O. Box 1576
San Bernardino, CA 92402

Cover illustration by Bruce Day.
Cover design by Michelle Treiber.

Upon the release of each new book, Here's Life Publishers sponsors the planting of a tree through Global ReLeaf ™, a program of the American Forestry Association.

Library of Congress Cataloging-in-Publication Data
      Hunt, Gary.
      Too young to drive, too old to ride : surviving your child's middle school
years / Gary and Angela Hunt.
            p.   cm.
      Includes bibliographical references.
      ISBN 0-89840-357-X
      1. Child rearing—United States. 2. Parent and child—United States.
3. Middle school students—United States. I. Hunt, Angela Elwell, 1957- . II. Title.
HQ769.H87   1992
649'.1—dc20   92-19562
                                                                              CIP

Unless indicated otherwise, Scripture quotations are from the *King James Version* of the Bible. Scripture quotations designated NKJ are from *The Holy Bible: New King James Version,* © 1982 by Thomas Nelson, Inc., Nashville, Tennessee. Scripture quotations designated NAS are from *The New American Standard Bible,* © The Lockman Foundation 1960, 1962, 1963, 1968, 1971, 1972, 1975, 1977.

For More Information, Write:
      L.I.F.E.—P.O. Box A399, Sydney South 2000, Australia
      Campus Crusade for Christ of Canada—Box 300, Vancouver, B.C., V6C 2X3, Canada
      Campus Crusade for Christ—Pearl Assurance House, 4 Temple Row, Birmingham, B2 5HG, England
      Lay Institute for Evangelism—P.O. Box 8786, Auckland 3, New Zealand
      Campus Crusade for Christ—P.O. Box 240, Raffles City Post Office, Singapore 9117
      Great Commission Movement of Nigeria—P.O. Box 500, Jos, Plateau State Nigeria, West Africa
      Campus Crusade for Christ International—100 Sunport Lane, Orlando, FL 32809, U.S.A.

We lovingly dedicate this book to our parents

Ron and Jean Hunt

and

James and Frankie Elwell

who saw us through our own tweenage years.

Author's Comments

We'd just like to say . . .

Most of the names mentioned in our stories have been changed. If there was a chance we'd cause embarrassment or any ill feeling from one of "our kids," we created a new name.

The English language can be awkward. Instead of referring constantly to "him or her" or "your son or daughter," we alternated between the sexes.

We owe a debt of gratitude to the kids who have let us enter their lives:

To the tweenagers who are now grown and married, we're unbelievably proud of you!

To those who are struggling through high school, remember we still love you. Give us a call sometime!

To those who are still in our department, be patient with us. We'll be telling *your* stories next year!

Contents

CONTENTS

A Time of Beginning and Expansion

Gary

Huntley was exasperated. I was driving him home from Sunday school, and as usual, was using the time to check up on how he was doing spiritually. Huntley had confessed that it was difficult to keep from cursing in school when his friends "cussed all the time."

"It's hard, Coach," he explained. "You gotta understand—I'm going through pooberty."

Angie and I had a good laugh over that one, but underlying Huntley's explanation was a solid fact: Going through puberty is not easy. Adolescence, strictly speaking, begins at puberty, but the rites of passage from childhood to adulthood begin when a child leaves elementary school and enters the neighborhood middle or junior high school.

It is in the middle school that a child becomes aware of older, more sophisticated preteens and teenagers. It is in the middle school that childhood toys are abandoned for record albums and designer clothes. It is the approach of middle school that leaves parents bewildered and confused.

I have pastored middle school students since 1975. While other pastors shudder at the thought of serving so long in such a position, I enjoy my work more each year. Parents who have sent two or three kids through our department will shake my hand and mutter, "I don't know how you do it."

How I do it is not as important as *why* I do it. I serve middle school students because these in-between years are crucial. It is during this time that most kids go through their "ugly duckling" stage. When self-esteem is lowest, the pressures of life are greatest.

If you are a parent, teacher or youth worker, I hope you will read this book with the pages of your memory open to the time when you were on the brink of maturity, poised for action but bereft of social skills, confidence and even the most basic physical coordination. To the time when being "in" meant everything. To the time when you'd rather be dead than be seen somewhere with your parents. To the time when you were too young to drive, but too old to ride.

My own junior high years are vividly brought back every Sunday morning. When they enter our middle school Sunday school department as sixth graders, the boys have high voices, scrawny arms and legs, and scurry from classroom to bathroom in groups of three and four. The girls enter with a roll of baby fat, frilly dresses and a shy demeanor.

On promotion Sunday in June our new sixth graders sing loudly and lustily. It takes only a week or two for them to pick up on the self-conscious air which pervades the atmosphere, however, and soon our song leader once again will be pumping his arms like a crazed whooping crane, appreciating even a meager response from the crowd.

Ah, the sixth graders! They sit quietly, unobtrusively, in small groups of two and three. They are observant, obedient and dutiful. They learn Bible verses as easily as they learn their friends' phone numbers, and they enthusiastically join in games, quizzes and anything with hoopla.

The seventh graders are another category altogether. They have a year's experience in middle school to their credit, and they strut into the room like rowdy peacocks. The girls greet each other with loud squeals of approval, exclaim over each other's dresses, and reserve long rows of chairs for their groups of friends. During the singing they shyly whisper the words of the songs as they look to their friends for support and shared giggles.

The boys wait outside the door until their buddies have arrived, then they enter with a rush of energy. Seventh grade boys fidget during the singing and fidget during the lesson. They make paper airplanes out of handouts and slyly try to annoy the "uncool" kids in the front of the room by flinging spitballs or paperwads.

What a transformation occurs between the seventh and eighth grades. Sudden sophistication! Overnight cool! Somehow, magically over the summer, the eighth grade girls seem to grow within an inch of their adult height. They wear clothing that would rival any career woman's wardrobe; they carry handbags to match their Sunday pumps. Makeup is applied carefully and colorfully; their hair is blow-dried, curled and firmly set in place with mousse, setting gel or hairspray—whatever happens to be the element of choice that season.

These "matrons" of our middle school department glide into the room with ease and confidence. They greet their friends with a slow smile, turn once or twice to discreetly display their outfits, and after checking with a friend to see which row of chairs has been appropriately reserved, seek out their seats with all the confidence of a titled lady approaching the royal box. Confidence, grace, and a certain upper-class attitude simply ooze from them.

During the class, these girls sit quietly, only occasionally taking glances at the section of chairs occupied by the eighth grade boys. These boys haven't made as drastic a change as the girls, but they, too, are aware of their new-found influence as eighth graders. Their hair is cut just-so; their outfits carefully chosen to exhibit either an air of Sunday dash or Saturday flash. Few of the eighth graders sing. Even fewer have the inclination to learn memory verses.

What has happened to those sweet little sixth graders who were reluctant to retire their Cabbage Patch dolls from active duty? Regardless of whether or not physical puberty has arrived, the middle school mentality has led them from childhood to adolescence, from an end to a beginning. As adolescence is the bridge between childhood and adulthood, so the middle school years are the bridge between childhood and adolescence.

Middle school students, ages ten to thirteen, are not children but not yet fully teenagers. These "tweenagers," as Angie and I like to call them, have unique needs, and you will find special considerations helpful as you parent or work with them. This is a rewarding area of ministry, an invisible investment which can lay a firm foundation for the times of testing and temptation ahead. Come with us as we explore and enjoy this much-ignored "tweenage."

1

Tweenagers in a Word? Extreme!

Angie

All adolescents are, in a sense, psychotic.
—Fanita English

Nicki came to Sunday school with glitter in her hair. Mike swaggered in with the haircut his mother begged him not to get. Jaysen sat in a corner proudly belching. Jessica burst through the door and ran to tug on Gary's sleeve. Her latest life-or-death crisis was that she saw one of her friends smoking in the school's rest room. What were we going to do about it?

Parents, if your ten-to-fourteen-year-old sounds like one of these children, don't despair. He or she has not developed a sudden case of insanity; this is simply a stage. Like temper tantrums and teething, this too will pass.

Tweenagers react against the symbols of both childhood and adulthood. They form their own bizarre subculture with extremes in every area: Their clothing is of the wildest color and style; their music contains the heaviest beat and most outlandish acts; their heroes are wildly worshipped; and their peer group is the most set in its conformity.

I remember a cartoon I read sometime during the 1970s. A bearded, long-haired, blue-jeaned peacenik stood before his father and pleaded: "But Dad, I've *got* to be a non-conformist. How else can I be like everybody else?"

Erase the beard and change the long hair to what today's fashions are and you have the perfect picture of a tweenager. "But Mom and Dad," we hear kids saying, "we've got to be different from you. How else can we be like kids?"

Should you let your son have pink hair? Should you let your daughter listen to heavy metal rock groups that bite off the heads of rats in performances? Should you let your daughter *or* son have three pierced holes in her or his ears?

Gauge each behavior by biblical standards. If the behavior is not a cultural symbol of rebellion and if it can be done and God still glorified, then let your tween express himself or herself.

Be prepared for anything—the tweenage years are the age of the *extreme*.

Extreme Hero Worship

I'll never forget one Sunday morning a few years ago. We had a musical team from our local college in to do a presentation, and one of their skits included a reference to Michael Jackson, who was then at a peak in his popularity.

Several of our "bus kids" were seated down front. These were nice kids who came on the church bus every Sunday and rarely gave us a moment's trouble. True, they never seemed to pay much attention and we couldn't see why they bothered to come at all since they roamed the halls much of the time, but they came without fail and always chose front-row, center seats.

When one of the performing college students broke out in a portrayal of Michael Jackson, a hornet's nest broke loose in the front section. One girl stood up, exclaiming loudly, "Michael doesn't look anything like that!" Another yelled, "Don't you act like that!"

When the startled college student started to speak, he was cut off by still another girl, "You hush up!" Jackson's loyal fans stood up and huffed out of the room, all because an unfortunate worker attempted to take the name of Michael Jackson in vain.

Strong hero worship is a trait of tweenagers, and it can be used in the ministry and in parenting if the young person is presented with heroes worthy of emulation.

One Sunday morning we had a guest teacher who asked the 300 middle schoolers in our class for a response to his question: "Who are your heroes?" When no one answered, he ventured out into the rows of kids, calling on students individually.

"Who is your hero?" he asked one student.

"Michael Jordan," the boy replied.

"Who is your hero?" he asked a girl.

"Amy Grant."

"Who is your hero?" he asked another boy.

The boy paused a moment and thought. "I guess Gary Hunt is," he answered. Imagine! The boy chose his youth pastor for a hero!

Any pastor should be worthy of hero worship from those he leads. Not only does a pastor or leader represent spiritual authority, but he is also a friend, a counselor, a teacher and a helper. In many situations he may also be a substitute parental figure. Even kids from "good" homes will look for what psychologists call "the significant other," a person outside the family circle who provides leadership and affirmation.

Extreme Avoidance of Parents

"Our family has always been close," one woman told me. "We've always enjoyed doing things together, but lately I get the feeling our thirteen-year-old daughter would rather spend time with *anyone* but us. She actually seemed embarrassed to be seen with us at a restaurant last week! I felt so hurt. Was I wrong to feel this way?"

Parents, your child has not outgrown her need or her love for you—it is the adult/baby role she has outgrown. She's embarrassed to be seen in public with you. She'd rather drop into a bottomless pit than let her friends see her mother holding up a shirt to her chest while shopping. When you drop your tween off at the mall for an afternoon with her friends, don't be surprised if she asks to be let out at the far corner. *She is simply embarrassed to be seen having her parents do something for her which she cannot yet do for herself.*

I remember well my own junior high days. I was involved in the science program and the concert choir, and whenever concert contests or science fairs came around, I was thrilled that I could travel for a day or two and be independent and away from my parents. It wasn't that I disliked or didn't respect them—it was simply great to be on my own. I was free to order what I wanted in restaurants, check into a hotel with my friends (and a chaperon lurking around the corner), and just be on my own for a while. If my parents were able to drive and meet me at the site, I doubt that I even spoke to them until I reluctantly rejoined them back at the school when the event was over. I was glad that they cared enough to come and see me perform, but I simply preferred to mix, mingle, and be seen on my own or with my friends.

Heartless? Now I think so, but then I felt independent and rather sophisticated. Eighth graders, you see, know everything.

Louise Ames has noticed that tweenagers not only

retreat from their families in public, but in private too. "At thirteen," she writes, "the child withdraws complete- ly from the family, both physically and emotionally. Very often, except at mealtimes, there is no sign of the thirteen- year-old around the house, since most of his time is spent alone in his room. And Thirteens tend not only to keep their room door closed, but also locked."[1]

This desire to be alone and independent is natural and provides the foundation for the independence you will want your child to have in later years.

Some children are more independent than others (particularly first-born children), and this desire for inde- pendence manifests itself at different times for each child.

Becky and Sarah, two tweenage sisters, went off to church camp for one week. Becky, the oldest girl, loved every minute and was disgruntled to return home. Sarah, who had not been able to join in the camp activities with the same enthusiasm as Becky, cried herself to sleep every night from homesickness and was thrilled to be back with mom and dad.

Their mother admitted that Sarah's homesickness was flattering. "I was relieved that Sarah missed us and annoyed that Becky didn't," she said.

But the girls' father understood his daughters' be- haviors: "Becky is more responsible and more ready to be independent," he said. "She has had more oppor- tunities to grow up and is closer to being the strong Christian woman we'd like her to be someday. It isn't bad that Sarah was homesick; we just need to realize that the girls are far apart in social development."

As the invisible umbilical cord between parents and children stretches thin, tweenagers begin to form other relationships. They establish their places in a peer group, reach out for new adult influences, and begin to open themselves to a host of friendships. Many parents are jealous of the affection their children lavish upon new adult friends such as youth workers, teachers or neigh-

bors. Parents often feel overlooked and underap-
preciated. They are deeply hurt when their kids obviously prefer the company of some new and more exciting
adult.

Extreme Crushes

As tweenagers seek new adult influences, boys and
girls sometimes develop passionate emotional attach-
ments to older women and men. Though boys do not
often develop a crush on an older woman (and when they
do, rarely do they do anything about it other than
daydream), most girls go through at least one mad crush
on an older male figure.

My husband and I have noticed that girls who have
no father in the home or who have an "absentee" father
are especially prone to develop a crush on a youth leader.
Personally, I'd much rather have my daughter develop a
crush on her youth pastor than on the latest rock singer,
but parents who are concerned about these "affairs of the
heart" can be assured that they are harmless unless un-
naturally encouraged.

We have an old bureau in our garage in which we
store odds and ends and bits and pieces of our lives. The
bottom drawer is crammed full of cards, sentimental
letters and notes from tweenagers of years past. Those
notes, handwritten and invariably folded into tiny football shapes or intricate self-envelopes, always remind us
of just how passionate and innocent is that first case of
hero worship. Here are a couple from our collection:

Gary:
I'm not mad, just upset. I feel like you don't care
about me. I know you do but you hardly ever spend
any time with me. I love you and I want you to love
me back. I know you do, I think, and if you do you
don't show it very much.

Dear Gary:

I love you very, very, very, very much. How have you been doing? Have you ever gotten mad or upset at me? Why? Please tell me. It would mean a lot to me. Have I ever hurt your feelings? If I have ever, forgive me because I am sorry! How have you been doing mentally, physically, spiritually? I'm sorry that I don't have any fancy writing paper. Well I just wanted to say "hi" and I love you! Keep on praying for me!

These may sound like ardent love letters, and in a sense they are. But these girls are just learning about the rush of feeling that "love" brings, and they are in love with the emotion more than anything else. Furthermore, their definition of "love" does not contain the element of sexuality that is inherent in an adult relationship.

Help Your Tween Through "First Love"

What do you do if your tweenage daughter develops a severe crush on an older or inappropriate male figure? First, talk to her and find out exactly who this person is. Try not to assume the role of an interrogator or make quick, harsh judgments about the object of your child's affection. Simply listen and try to understand. If you laugh, fuss or decide to ignore the state of affairs, your daughter will reason, "My parents simply don't understand. Why did I ever think they could?"

Do not forbid the feelings—your child will simply say, "I can't control my emotions!" Then her feelings will not only be passionate, but desperately passionate.

After you know with whom your daughter is infatuated, judge whether this person can be trusted around your adoring daughter. If he is a responsible adult, don't worry, but continue to be cautious. If he is an adult with whom you are not acquainted, get to know him. Go for a visit and say, "My daughter thinks a lot of you and I wanted to meet you." If he is aware that your daughter has a crush on him, he will wisely continue to be nice, but not too encouraging.

Make sure your child isn't spending unreasonable amounts of time with this person, and try to make sure they are not spending unsupervised time alone. Never assume anyone is totally harmless. Even youth pastors and teachers who may need to privately counsel your daughter should have other people around.

But if the crush amounts to nothing but "sighing" from afar, let it go. Scores of girls have had crushes on my husband, and we've seen their feelings grow from first love to a fatherly appreciation. He has performed the wedding ceremonies of many of those girls, and now they have established homes of their own.

Extreme Activity

All tweenagers, boys and girls, gravitate to adults who are exciting and fun. Those who work with tweenagers should recognize this and make sure activities planned for this age group are fast-paced, colorful and well-planned. If you are planning a party for your tweenage kid, you can't go wrong if you make food your highest priority. The best food? Pizza! It is fast, filling and self-serve; just be sure there is plenty of it. I've seen one junior high boy eat an entire large pizza in fifteen minutes.

Our senior high school department annually sponsors a Hawaiian luau. They painstakingly plan decorations, costumes, games and an elaborate menu. The outdoor site of the luau takes a week to prepare; the food is cooked days ahead; and special music and lots of little "extras" are provided—a souvenir program, leis for all who attend, background Hawaiian music during the dinner itself.

All of the above would be wasted on junior highers. Tweenagers give only a cursory glance to decorations; the programs would inevitably be folded into paper airplanes; the boys would refuse to wear flowers; and the Hawaiian music would be drowned out during dinner by belching and scuffling. The best activity for tweenagers is something fast and physical. Take your tweenagers skating, feed them pizza, and you'll be a hero.

Extreme Humor

Many adults would be slightly sickened by the sight of a room in which tweenagers have just eaten. *Any* adult would be nauseated by a full dose of the gastronomical humor which comes naturally to tweenage boys. Tweenage humor, to the adult mind, is perverted.

This is the age when bodily functions are outrageously funny and food is not only meant to be eaten but chewed, played with, displayed, barfed and re-eaten. To the young adolescent mind, the grossest jokes (or sights or sounds) are the funniest.

There are times when *everything* is funny to a tweenager. Thomas Cottle, writing in *12 to 16*, remembers his own early adolescent years:

> We laughed at styles of appearance and voice, and, best of all, tangible deformity drove us into hysterics. Knowing it was dreadful of us, we nonetheless could rarely contain ourselves if we caught a buddy's eyes in class or while riding a bus. Someone would be overly fat, or tall, or dressed differently, or have long hair, or slip on a stair, or ask a bus driver in "broken" English for the location of a street, and we would look and listen intently and then, blam, we would be busting with the pains of laughter, the tears rolling down our cheeks, and grappling to catch some inner strand or throw a switch that might bring us back to normalcy.[2]

Extreme Manners—The Verbal Jest

Tweenagers are masters of the "put-down"—particularly if the cut is on someone else. While a tweenager's self-esteem is usually incredibly fragile, he enjoys nothing more than hearing his best friend or youth leader cut to ribbons. My husband has a bald spot on the top of his head and a sure way for another worker to win the "respect" of our kids is to make a cutting remark about Gary's bald spot.

Tweenagers love to hear sarcastic humor because they are tremendously self-conscious. They are awkward and insecure and, more than anything, they fear public embarrassment. When a youth pastor or worker gets a public cut, they laugh along in relief and devilish joy that someone else is on the hot seat for the moment.

Youth workers, however, use the put-down on kids at their own risk. Calling a kid "chicken lips" in public may win a laugh, but it may also alienate that kid forever. Youth workers should be sure that the kid who is an object of a joke has enough self-assurance to handle the public attention and knows that no harm is intended.

There are always some kids who are upset when the youth pastor or worker *doesn't* tease them—they feel left out of the camaraderie. But keep in mind that tweenagers are hypersensitive and what may be a joke to you can be a serious blow to an insecure young person.

Parents, a word of advice: Don't use the put-down with your kids (or with each other). "Gosh," one girl told me after I counseled her about her low self-image, "even my mother says I'm a klutz." The mother may have been playfully joking, but the words remained in her daughter's mind. *If your parents don't stick up for you,* kids reason, *who will?*

Put-Downs in Anger

Often tweenagers let loose with a string of put-downs more in anger than in jest. They are using the put-down as self-defense, a form of verbal fighting which often leads to physical aggression. Virtually every fist fight between boys starts with a verbal insult.

How do we help tweenagers keep a guard on their tongues? First, *we* must make the resolution never to put down a child in anger. Our speech needs to be positive. As parents, when our children need rebuking, never criticize the child—correct the action.

"You are stupid, lazy and dumb!" shouted Joe's father. "We do everything for you and you don't have the gratitude to do a simple thing like taking out the garbage when we asked you to!"

A wiser father would have said, "Son, because you went off without putting the garbage out, your mother and I were late for an important appointment. Your action was thoughtless. I know you can do better."

Tweenagers need praise and affirmation, not criticism and condemnation. By controlling our own tongues and emphasizing the biblical teaching on the tongue (James 1:26; 3:1-12; and the book of Proverbs), we can teach our children to cultivate wholesome, productive speech.

Extreme Energy

You may have noticed that tweens often have trouble controlling their bodies. Aside from the awkwardness which accompanies rapid growth, Edward Martin, who taught junior high students for several years, noticed a "general twitchiness" among his students. "Movement was the standard," he relates, "tapping of hands or fingers, wiggling bodies, turning heads, bouncing, jiggling, squirming. These were not the exuberant and free movements of small children, nor the coordinated and powerful movements of youth, but rather an uncontrolled display and use of body."[3]

Extreme—But Fleeting—Commitments

Martin also noticed the instant and complete commitment of tweenagers to a person, idea, activity or event:

> Four months after I had stopped teaching a particular group of seventh grade students, I appeared in the school lunch room where many from the class were eating. A cry went up "There's Mr. Martin!" and suddenly I was surrounded by eight bubbling girls and boys all talking at once, all asking a string of questions about where I was and what I was doing. By the time I had recovered from the charge and my ego had hopelessly swelled, I realized I was alone again. The eight had returned to their other activities just as fast as they had come.[4]

Are you ready for the extreme world of the tweenager?

2

Preparing for Adolescence

Angie

My mother had a great deal of trouble with me,
but I think she enjoyed it.
—Mark Twain

Dear Meg,
       Yesterday we packed away the remnants of your childhood. You are almost thirteen, and you said it was time. So down into the storage room went your dollhouse, cradle, and games—all the toys that said, "This is a little girl's room." You wanted to hang posters, stack tapes, make your room look more grownup . . .
       What this means, my almost teenager, is that over the next few years you will be amazed at how little your dad and I know about what's in, out or cool. There's a good chance that if we like something, you'll hate it; that when we chat with your friends, we'll embarrass you; that when we say no to an activity, you will quickly inform us that every other teenager in America is allowed to do it.

As a result, at times you will think we are the dumbest, meanest, most unfair parents on earth. And that's okay, I guess, because we love you enough to risk your not always liking us . . . [1]

Don't Dread Adolescence

My high school English teacher gave me the key to writing a good expository theme: "Tell 'em what you're gonna tell 'em, then tell 'em, then tell 'em what you told 'em." If you want to peacefully survive the tweenage years, first learn what's going to happen, then watch it happen, then reflect (and rejoice!) on what happened. It's a natural process and one you can learn from. These years may be difficult, but, to quote the old mountain climber, it's the bumps in life you climb on!

What can parents do to prepare themselves and their children for the onset of the tweenage years?

First, don't dread the adolescent years. They are natural and normal and can be fun and exciting! You are not losing your dutiful son or daughter—you are gaining a young person on the road to independence. You are beginning the most crucial building program you have ever undertaken.

What man plans to build a lovely home and then dreads the actual building process? Suppose a couple plans to build their dream home. For years they carefully save every extra dollar and search through house plans and pictures. When they are financially able, they choose exactly the right lot after months of careful surveying. After weeks of further planning, they hire a contractor, finalize their house plans and arrange a date for the foundation to be poured.

This couple knows the actual building process may take two or three months, but their lovely home will be worth the wait. Why should they be nervous about beginning to build? Building can be fun! They have planned well, and they trust their builder. There is no reason why their home will not be a success.

Seeing a child through adolescence is not much different. If you plan for the tweenage years and trust the Master Builder, the finished creation will be a glorious success. There is no need to fear the years ahead.

So what's the plan?

Communicate With Respect and Consideration

The Smiths and their son, Jonathan, were driving home from church. "What was your lesson about today, Jon?" drilled his mother.

Jon felt like he was under examination. He was dismally reminded of a harsh teacher at school, but he quietly mumbled, "Nothing much."

"Nothing?" queried his father. "You didn't get anything out of the lesson? Didn't you listen?"

"Yes, I listened!" snapped Jon. "It was just the old story about Daniel and the lions' den. I've heard it a million times."

"I tell you, Dear," said Mr. Smith to Mrs. Smith, "these kids aren't learning anything. Someone isn't doing his job. Perhaps I should speak to the pastor about Jon's Sunday school teacher."

Meanwhile, the Johnsons were driving home with their son, Tim. "Did you enjoy the lesson today, Tim?" asked his mother.

"Yeah, it was okay," replied Tim. "The story of Daniel and the lions' den."

"That was always my favorite story," remarked Mr. Johnson. "I always thought if I could have half as much courage as Daniel, I'd do okay in the world."

"What do you think, Tim?" asked Mrs. Johnson. "Would you like to be as courageous as Daniel?"

"Sure. Maybe then I'd have the guts to tell the guys in my science class to stop giving the teacher a hard time.

I could do a lot of things if I had that kind of courage."

"Well, Tim," his mother replied, "what's to stop you from having Daniel's courage? You know the same God."

Instead of verbally attacking your tweenager like the Smiths, encourage creative responses. Talk to your child with the same good manners and consideration you'd give another adult.

When your child was younger, the adult/child role was appropriate. Now, however, your child is assuming his own independence, and you should not continue to talk to him like a child.

Some of the most effective children's workers I know are people who simply acknowledge that children exist. When you meet a couple with their little children in tow, do you take the time to greet the children after you've greeted their parents? Do you talk about your children's personal problems when your children are standing nearby, as if they can't hear you? Children, even tweenagers, are accustomed to being "talked down to" or ignored by adults.

Talk to your children as loving leaders, not as drill sergeants. You'll find that a little respect goes a long way.

Involve Your Child in Creative Thinking

When you need to discipline your child, ask for his input. "What do you think it would take for you to learn this lesson?" a parent could ask.

When your daughter comes home from school and tells you that Mary and Susie are fighting because Mary misunderstood what Susie meant when she said Stephanie liked Jeff more than Mary, ask your daughter what could have been done to ease the situation without fighting and anger. Encourage your tween to express her ideas and opinions.

Get to Know the Adults in Your Child's Life

Historically, young teenagers were quickly assigned to apprenticeships where older and wiser adults guided them through the transition from childhood to maturity. This adult relationship provided the bridge upon which the child passed into responsible adulthood. Sadly, even though young people are crying out for adults to emulate, there are few adults today who have the time or inclination to invest their lives in young people. Seeking that outside influence, tweenagers often find that the peer group is their only bridge to adulthood. The peer group does not offer the wisdom, experience, responsibility or knowledge young people need, but it does offer acceptance.

If your child is fortunate during his tweenage years, he will be able to establish friendships with adults apart from you, his parents. Up until this time his adult acquaintances have been your friends, but during the tweenage years children begin to seek out individual adult relationships. These friendships may be established with favorite teachers or coaches, youth pastors, a neighbor or a Scout master. Not all of these relationships will be beneficial; some may even be dangerous. Get to know, at least on an informal basis, the other adults with whom your child interacts.

The youth workers in your church have a special job—to oversee the spiritual life of your child during these crucial years. Take the time to meet and talk with your child's youth pastor or Sunday school teacher. There may be a time when he or she will need your input or help.

A good youth worker supports parents, recognizes that all families are different, and keeps the lines of communication open between parents, tweenagers and the church.

Help Your Child Adjust
to His New School Situation

Whether your community offers junior high schools or middle schools, your tweenager will face huge adjustments as he goes from being the "big man on campus" at an elementary school to junior high. You can help your child with this adjustment in several ways.

First, go with your son or daughter to open house or registration and quietly walk through the halls with your tween to locate his locker and classrooms. Make sure he knows his locker combination. Get a map of the school and study it together. Get your daughter a bra (whether she needs one or not) so she'll fit in with the other girls who change clothes for physical education. Let her shave her legs.

Make sure your child leaves his childhood lunchbox at home. Lunch in middle school is best carried in a plain brown bag. Watch the other kids and see how they're carrying their books to school—in a duffel bag, backpack or just in a loose pile? Make sure your tweenager can blend in comfortably.

When your child comes home and says that "everyone" is wearing a certain item of clothing, make an effort to help your child fit in. If you can only purchase one of the specific item, be prepared to wash it several times a week. If you simply can't afford it, help your tweenager find a way to earn the money himself. He may decide that the status symbol isn't worth it.

Some Christians might feel it is wrong to allow children to mirror the clothing and styles of their peers. There are certain symbols of rebellion we don't want our children to pick up, but other things may be quite harmless. Is your child's self-esteem worth an overpriced $40 tee shirt? Only you and your child can answer that question.

Ask your youth pastor or pastor to introduce your

tweenager to other Christian kids who will be attending the same school. Even though they may not have classes together, they can see each other in the halls and take comfort from knowing there is at least one Christian friend at school with them. Several tweenagers in our church have begun before-school prayer meetings on their middle school campuses. They meet once a week to support and pray for one another, and the resulting sense of solidarity helps them feel a little less lost when school becomes overwhelming.

Expect a Change of Identity

In sixth grade I was known as Angela Elwell. I wore my hair short, pulled tightly with a barrette to one side of my head. I had buck teeth and was the only one in my class who still wore anklet socks with my tennis shoes. I made straight *A's* and favored the library over outdoor activities. My teachers were my best friends.

In the seventh grade I decided to change myself. I began calling myself "Angie" and writing my "t's" the old-fashioned way, without a crossbar and with the upward swoop at the end of a word. I found two other best friends; we became a threesome. I loosened up—gone were the ankle socks and the barrette, and my grades began to include some *B's*. Braces took care of the buck teeth. I stopped wearing my cousin's hand-me-downs and began to sew some of my own clothes. Friends, and acceptance, had become more important than the library and my teachers.

Today I still cross my "t's" the old-fashioned way, and my close friends still call me Angie. The changes I consciously made in the seventh grade have, for the most part, remained.

Your child, too, will probably change some part of his identity. He will shuck off the identity you have given him as easily as he discards the clothes you buy him.

Some of these passing phases will be incorporated into the person he will ultimately become; others will fade away. I went through an "I-am-an-animal-lover" phase and my mother had to cope with breeding gerbils, two baby chicks, kittens, a dog, a parakeet and my intense desire for baby rabbits. (Only the dog and a parakeet are in my household today.) Tweenagers simply "try on" different identities to see which ones suit them best.

Along with this search for identity comes the accompanying fear that the person inside will not measure up to the accepted standard. Each tweenager wrestles with two sets of characteristics: an unchangeable physical set (hair and eye color, body size, facial features) and a much larger, intangible set which can only be defined by comparison with his peers. Jerome Kagan says the latter set "includes adjectives like intelligent, wise, athletic, brave, pretty, confident, independent, responsible and sociable. Assignment to positions on these dimensions, by adult or child, requires the slippery judgement of comparison."[2]

Help Your Child Discover Who He Is

Tweenagers are labeled by peers, family, church workers, teachers and even physicians. Often labels are applied too soon, and a child never realizes that he or she could outgrow or outperform a negative label.

Labels have surprising staying power. I remember Donald Shockey, who was labeled our class "brain" in the sixth grade. Donald lived up to his name, ultimately graduating near the top of our high school class. (Everyone was amazed when someone else turned out to be valedictorian.) Though Donald was good-looking, no one ever considered him a "hunk" because he was the "brain."

When I took my first teaching job I replaced a teacher who had left two weeks into the school year. My students were unknown to me, and I graded their first essays with a strict and impartial eye. When I handed Andrea's paper back to her, she turned pale and I thought she might faint. You see, Andrea was the brain of her class and no teacher had ever given her less than a 95. I had given her essay a 93! She spent an hour after class with me, thoroughly probing my grading system so she would never fall short again.

How can you help a tweenager as he begins to discover his own identity? Bruce B. Barton has outlined several suggestions:

1. Prevent premature closure. Avoid using labels such as "You're no good at math," "You're great in sports," or "You'll probably be a preacher." We have to keep reminding our children that they are worth infinitely more to God than any evaluation parents or friends pin on them.

2. Expose tweens to various constructive and healthy adult role models. Perhaps they can work at a summer camp or get a job with a relative.

3. Remember to show joy and pleasure in your life and work and in your adult sexuality. Don't allow your tween to believe that people die emotionally when they reach age twenty-one.

4. Help kids arrange priorities for their capabilities. Some children have more than one interest or ability. A child may like softball, biology, church work and computers. That doesn't mean he has to be a Christian, softball-playing, computer-biologist. It is possible to develop some abilities as hobbies and still others as occasional interests.

5. Grant recognition by giving honest approval for the things they do well. Help them to recognize and see their strengths in skills, knowledge and attitudes.

6. Screen your own expectations of them. Make sure you are not prompting them toward something that is out of their depth.

7. Reassure them and yourself that adolescence does involve some suffering.

8. Talk about your Christianity. Describe your own life experiences that have brought you to your conclusions. Use the principle of pointing rather than telling. Give your tween the opportunity to draw his own conclusions and to challenge and disagree with you. Urge him to back up what he says.

9. Above all, make sure that during this time period you build up their identity in Christ rather than their identity based on how well they perform. So many people judge other persons on appearance or performance rather than as human beings loved and created by God.[3]

I used to have a youth pastor who made each of us memorize this slogan:

I!
I am!
I am me!
I am me and I am good!
I am me and I am good because God don't make no junk!

It seems silly now, but whenever things were rough growing up or whenever I had been hurt by another person, I used to mumble under my breath, "I! I am! I am me! I am me and I am good! . . . " Believe me—it worked!

Teach your tweenagers something they can fall back on when times get rough. As parents, assure them that the love you feel for them goes beyond "I love you because you're my kid." Specify and name positive character attributes that you love and appreciate in your child. You'll help him discover who he really is.

If you work with young people, be willing to be the significant adult friend in a tweenager's life. With your friendship for support, strong loving parents, and the knowledge that God loves them deeply and personally, tweenagers will be well on their way to finding a wholesome identity.

Respect Your Child's Desire for Privacy

It is during the tweenage years that your child's bedroom door will be closed for hours on end. "What is she doing in there?" a parent may wonder. Don't worry. Your daughter may be reading, dreaming, writing, gazing into the mirror or examining her rapidly-changing body. Allow her time for introspection.

Your tweenager may be an introvert. Forcing her to participate in group activities when she is unsure of herself will only accentuate the differences between her shyness and the boisterous attitude of others. Give your child room to find herself.

Don't Withhold Physical Affection

Although your child may pull away in embarrassment and may blush, keep giving those hugs of approval and affection. Just don't do it in front of "the guys."

Let your child set the boundaries for physical contact. A self-conscious tween will not be as eager to receive those hugs and kisses as the seven-year-old you once knew, but it's not necessary to avoid all physical affection. Respect your child's limits, all the while assuring him of your faithful support and love.

Give Your Child the Freedom to Make Decisions

A college student I recently counseled moaned,

"I've never had a job and I've never had a budget. I'd like to get out of school but I have no place to go but home, no money, and no skills. I wouldn't even know how to begin to balance a checkbook."

This young woman is unfortunate. Her parents never gave her the opportunity or the responsibility of providing anything for herself. Everything she needed was given to her; she was accountable for nothing.

You can begin to develop your child's autonomy in late elementary school. You might begin by allowing your child to choose his own school clothes within a certain budget. Soon you might give him an allowance for school supplies and teach him how to spend wisely on the things he will need.

When children enter early adolescence, they should be able to responsibly handle minor decisions regarding their friends, music, activities, wardrobe, schoolwork and hobbies. Give them the freedom to decide for themselves while you are there to help them.

Keep Your Marriage Strong

Adolescence is difficult enough without battling the grief and guilt of a broken home. No matter how amicable a divorce may be, psychologists have noted that nearly all children see themselves as the reason for the breakup of the family.

Take the time to keep your marriage strong. Spend quiet time alone with your spouse and recapture the romance of your marriage. Show by example how a Christian man and woman conduct themselves lovingly and respectfully in a marriage ordained by God. Your example may be the best reason your child will have for maintaining high moral standards when she begins to date and to seek her life's partner.

Take a few moments to talk with your tweenager about marriage. By casually asking, "What sort of person do you want to marry?" and continuing the discussion, you can begin to instill the values your child will need for a solid foundation when he or she begins to seriously consider marriage.

Have Fun as a Family

"Family Together Night" is an idea whose time has come. In a day when fathers and mothers work and children are busier than ever with school activities, families often fracture into individuals with separate agendas.

Set aside one night for the family. Keep the calendar clear of all other events, including church, television, work and school commitments. Search through idea books for fun activities and educational ventures that will be entertaining for the entire family. If the age span of your children is broad, have the children take turns selecting an activity for the family. A family is a team, and no team can expect to be successful without practice, communication and an exuberant team spirit.

Lead Your Child to Christ at an Early Age

Children of seven and eight are able to understand spiritual conditions and make a commitment to their faith. Statistics indicate that relatively few people make a commitment to Christ after age twelve, and the odds against a salvation decision grow greater with each passing year.

When I interviewed Dr. Clyde Narramore, the pioneer in the field of Christian psychology, he advised me on one of the best ways parents can show love to their children:

> Lead a child to the Lord at an early age and then help him to walk each day with God. Help him understand that God is the Creator of all things. Lead him in paths of righteousness. Explain everything in spiritual

terms as much as possible. Say, "Look at that tree. It's continually pumping water to its many parts. There's a wonderful pumping system inside the tree. Do you know who put it there? The Lord did."

Really, it doesn't take an awful lot of maturity to realize that you've done things that are wrong, that sin displeases God, and that God sent Jesus Christ to die for us. Children can use computers at three and four. They can know and do much by the time they are five. Consequently, they can understand the gospel at a very young age.

I think it may be detrimental to a person's intellect if he has to live in this world and not understand many basic facts such as sin, salvation, Christian growth and God's working throughout the world.[4]

Don't let your tweenagers go through the adolescent years spiritually unprepared. Rich spiritual knowledge can give your child wisdom beyond his years and see him through many difficult situations.

Making the Transition

The best preparation for the tweenage years and the launch of adolescence is a good parent/child relationship which has been nurtured throughout the childhood years. If you love your child and maintain open and honest communication, and if you place a strong emphasis on spiritual growth and development, your entrance into the tweenage years will be smoother.

Tweens Under Peer Pressure

Gary

Don't laugh at a youth for his affectations;
he's only trying on one face after another
till he finds his own.
—Logan Pearsall Smith

James Dobson, writing in *Parents and Teenagers*, reports the following:

> Dr. Urie Bronfenbrenner, eminent authority on child development at Cornell University, told a Senate committee that the junior high years are probably the most critical to the development of a child's mental health. It is during this period of self-doubt that the personality is often assaulted and damaged beyond repair. Consequently, said Bronfenbrenner, it is not unusual for healthy, happy children to enter junior high school, but then emerge two years later as broken, discouraged teenagers.

> I couldn't agree more emphatically with Bronfenbrenner's opinion at this point. Junior high

school students are typically brutal to one another, attacking and slashing a weak victim in much the same way a pack of northern wolves kill and devour a deformed caribou. Few events stir my righteous indignation more than seeing a vulnerable child—fresh from the hand of the Creator in the morning of his life—being taught to hate himself and despise his physical body and wish he had never been born.[1]

Tweenagers are the most insecure people in the world. The thing they ardently seek is often the most difficult and fleeting goal to pursue: status and approval from their peers.

What gives status? James S. Coleman studied 7,000 students in Illinois in 1957, and his findings are still valid today. Having high grades is not a basis for popularity among tweens, but being an athlete, being in the "leading crowd," and being a leader in activities are important to boys. Being in the leading crowd, being a leader in activities, and having nice clothes are most important to girls.[2]

This is the age of group conformity, and, fortunately, there are always several groups into which a tweenager may fit. Unfortunately, not all groups are accepted or given the "seal of approval." In our middle school department at church we have clearly defined cliques. There is a group of wealthy girls who dress like career women, a group of physically immature giggly girls, a punk group, a spiritual group, an athletic group, an apathetic group, a group of the juvenile delinquents of tomorrow, an in-between group, and a group of social misfits.

Where Cliques Come From

How do these groups form? Most children from families of similar social standing and wealth have similar interests, so it is natural that they gravitate toward each other. In fact, peer groups often reinforce parental values because a child is likely to choose peers from his own social, educational, economic and religious background. I have always been amazed at how quickly a new kid can find his appropriate peer group. They seem to have a special "radar."

Each school represented in our department has its own and more clearly defined version of the peer groups mentioned earlier. Edward Martin writes:

> One comes to school to see friends. One fears school because enemies are there also. Some of the most important parts of the school day are the walk or ride there, changing between classes, the few minutes before the class gets started, the study hall, and the end of school. These times are the intense periods of "seeing the other kids," or realizing you have no one to see.[3]

Influence of Peers—Bad and Good

Urie Bronfenbrenner has noted that the peer group has the potential for becoming a destructive force:

> At least in the United States, the peer group tends to undermine adult socialization efforts and to encourage egocentrism, aggression, and antisocial behavior.[4]

A large-scale survey of American sixth-graders found that those children who were the most peer-oriented were also those who reported engaging most often in antisocial activities such as lying to adults, smoking, and using bad language.[5]

Not only can peer groups promote undesirable behavior, but they are often responsible for repressing individual tastes, values and emotions. Many would-be musicians give up music during adolescence because time spent practicing is not as important as time spent with friends. Girls whose one beauty is their hair will cut it, perm it and tangle it if their friends are doing the same.

Clothes Make the Tween

Nicki was the queen bee in her clique. All the members of her group were well-dressed-designer-punk-public-school girls. I remember visiting her one hot August afternoon a week before school started. She had just returned from a visit to see her father. Nicki's parents were divorced, and her dad made every effort to spoil her on her semi-annual trips. She brought out several shopping bags to show me.

"Look at this jacket," she commanded. "It cost $55. These jeans are the latest from Italy," she said as she held them up. "Thirty-five dollars a pair and I've got three pairs."

She held up shoes, sweaters, jackets and skirts, mentioning the designer's name and the exact price of each item. I felt a little sorry for her mother who was working hard just to keep the modest home for the two of them. If she had bought Nicki a pair of plain-pocket jeans, I know Nicki would have refused to wear them.

On some Sunday mornings at church I will see groups of two or three tweens wearing different versions of the same outfit. I remember one Easter when a group of friends all wore pink pumps. "You can't sit in this row," I joked with one bewildered girl who had just come into the class. "This row is reserved for pink shoes."

The Pressure to Pair Off

Although the "group" is very important, older tweenagers also have a need to be accepted by the opposite sex—and by one member of the opposite sex in particular. The tweens we know call it "going together," but all I ever get is a blank look when I ask them, "Where are you going?"

"Oh, Gary," is the exasperated reply. "You know what we mean."

"Going together" or "going out" or whatever phrase

is popular with your tweens means that boy likes girl and girl likes boy back. They are too young to date, of course, and in our Sunday school guys and girls usually sit on opposite sides of the room. So what *do* they do? Well, the girls whisper about "her boy" and giggle a lot; the boys compliment him on his taste in women. If the young man is exceptionally brave, he may call her on the telephone once or twice. One of them will probably cross the great divide so they can sit together in Sunday school.

If any tweenage parties fall during the going together period, both will be invited and they may sit together. Occasionally chaperons may find them kissing or holding hands surreptitiously. If the youth group takes a bus trip, they will undoubtedly sit together and undoubtedly bear close watching. They do what they think they are expected to do, but they have little emotional maturity and even less experience to tell them what *not* to do.

How do we view coupling at this age when statistics indicate that twelve- and thirteen-year-olds are experimenting with sex? In most instances, going together is harmless and passes quickly.

"Twelve-year-olds," writes Edward Martin, "hang around in groups by sex. It is a rare exception when a member of one sex risks associating with members of the opposite sex."[6]

I have to believe, though, that a tweenager who is deeply upset and seeking either a father figure or love in any form could easily be led to experiment with sex. And of course it is not impossible for tweenagers to mimic what they see in movies and on television. But physical involvement is not a usual activity for tweenagers, particularly kids who have been reared in religious families.

Be firm with your child if he is "going" with someone. Make sure he knows about sex, its temptations and the progression which leads from affection to intercourse. Remind him that there is plenty of time for full-fledged dating, and feel free to limit opportunities for coupling.

Going together is the first taste of what is to come—a romantic relationship, his name linked with hers, a twosome, a sometimes-togetherness. It is thrilling, but at the same time it is a little unsettling and uncomfortable. Just remember that this, too, is a necessary part of growing up.

Possibility for Change

Friends mold and shape each other into mirror reflections of themselves, so peer pressure, or peer influence, can sometimes be a source for great good. Proverbs 27:17 tells us: "Iron sharpeneth iron; so a man sharpeneth the countenance of his friend." Strong Christian kids can influence their friends and encourage each other in right living.

But what can be done about the negative groups and their influence? Is there any hope for a girl or boy who wants out of an "anti-social" group?

Yes, there is. Groups change, often with astonishing rapidity. One fight over a boyfriend can send a girl scurrying from one peer group to another. Any change in a family's social status is impetus for a change of social group. If a boy or girl transfers from one school to another, he or she is certain to enter another peer group.

In fact, parents should be aware that tweenagers are the most vulnerable when they change schools. Often a kid who has never been a problem will strive to be accepted in his new school quickly. The quickest way to find peer acceptance is to attract attention—usually bad, noisy, disruptive or harmful attention. Other kids who see their wholesome lives as "boring" might decide to "change their image" and try something new. If your family is moving or if your tweenager will be changing schools, spend some extra time to ensure that your child is making a smooth transition.

Since change is possible, a wise parent or youth worker can really help a young person by seeing that they enter a group which is "on target" spiritually. You can't *dictate* this decision, but you can help in the decision-making process. If you have been teaching the principles of right and wrong rather than mandating dictatorial rules, your child will have the wisdom to discern which groups are "good" and which are "trouble." Talk to your tweenager about peer groups and how they help or hurt him. Keep your communication open and make sure your family plays an active part in your child's life.

Amy was involved with a group we call "apathetic." They sit with glum faces in Sunday school, refuse to participate in Bible memorization on Wednesday nights and generally let us know they're at church only because their parents force them to come.

Amy wanted out. She knew her friends were dragging her down spiritually, so she prayed about her situation and sought my counsel. Over the summer she was separated from her friends by a prolonged family vacation, and when the next school year began she made a conscious effort to enter a different group of girls.

Amy did well, but often I would see her struggling in Sunday school. Her old group would come in and sit behind her. As they wrote notes and quietly giggled, I could tell a part of her wanted to be with them—she wanted to talk about boys and clothes and fun, too. But Amy stuck it out and is now happy and settled with her new friends. Sure, her new friends talk about boys and clothes, but they have things in a better perspective.

How to Balance Peer Influence

Do all adolescents turn away from their parents and toward their peers at this time of life? Yes and no. Some breaking away from parental guidance and authority is natural and normal. But studies have shown that "the

peer-oriented child is more a product of parental dis-
regard than of the attractiveness of the peer group—that
[the child] turns to his age mates less by choice than by
default. The vacuum left by the withdrawal of parents
and adults from the lives of children is filled with an
undesired—and possibly undesirable—substitute of an
age-segregated peer group."[7]

Quite simply, parents who take an active part in
their children's lives by spending time with their children
will continue to have the primary influence in their
tweens' lives. When the relationship between parents
and children is strong, parental influence will exceed
peer influence. However, parents who let their children
withdraw from the family circle will allow the peer
relationship to become the most important influence in a
child's head and heart.

Daniel Yankelovich did a study in 1981 called "New
Rules." Former U. S. Secretary of Education William
Bennett remarked on the Yankelovich study:

> He [Yankelovich] found evidence of something
> that should distress all of us concerned about young
> people. He suggests in his study that parents began to
> put the raising of children at a lower priority in their
> lives. He describes what we might call a terrible com-
> pact, a deal. As he says in his report, "We shall demand
> less from you, children, and in return we'll make less
> sacrifice for you." Yankelovich talks about the statisti-
> cally demonstrable fact that many couples were less
> willing to stay together for the sake of their children
> during this period of 1960 to 1980. Yankelovich talks
> about an increasing tendency "for parents to say they
> wish to live their own lives, even if it means less time
> with their children."[8]

Parents must not give up their place of influence and
authority in their children's lives. Members of the White
House Conference on Children made the following discovery:

The young cannot pull themselves up by their own bootstraps. It is primarily through observing, playing, and working with others older and younger than himself that a child discovers both what he can do and who he can become—that he develops both his ability and his identity. It is primarily through exposure and interaction with adults and children of different ages that a child or adolescent acquires new interests and skills and learns the meaning of tolerance, cooperation, and compassion. Hence to relegate children to a world of their own is to deprive them of their humanity. Yet, this is what is happening in America today.[9]

What, then, is a parent to do? For starters, spend as much time as possible with your child. Begin to think of your tweenager as a very young adult and do as little as possible to embarrass him in public. In private, though, let your child know that you love him totally. Reach out for a hug even though he may pull away.

"Don't just listen while you're watching TV or reading the newspaper," says James Ventress, executive director of the Boys and Girls Clubs of America chapter in Santa Clarita, California. "Look at your child. Give him your full attention. You need to understand, not just to hear. Parents who exert that extra effort can make a major difference in their children's lives."[10]

Plan some special days for your son or daughter. Make popcorn at bedtime and eat it with your daughter in her room as you talk about school and friends. Mothers, let your son take you out for lunch on a Saturday afternoon. Slip him the money before you go and allow him to order for you and pay the bill. Fathers, take your daughter out to eat at an elegant restaurant. Show her how a gentleman treats a lady.

Making Wise Choices

But no matter how much time you spend with your

tweenager, there will be times when he or she will have to make a decision in the face of peer pressure. A recent poll by the Boys and Girls Clubs of America found that two-thirds of the 3282 teens surveyed felt considerable peer pressure to drink, take drugs and/or have sex. Forty percent felt pressure *not* to do well in school.[11]

How can you help your tween learn to make wise choices? It might help if you introduce the following guidelines for decision making to your tween:

1. Will doing this harm my body?

2. If I do this, will I be disobeying someone God has placed over me?

3. Will this decision help or hurt someone else?

4. Will I be glad I did this tomorrow?

5. If Jesus were standing beside me right now, could I do this?

Facing Fear and Disappointment

If your tween makes a brave and wise choice that goes against her "crowd," she may have to face unpleasant consequences. My favorite *Andy Griffith* episode is the one where Opie is being bullied by a kid who demands his milk money every morning on the way to school. Andy doesn't want to embarrass his son by taking up Opie's fight, but he doesn't want to see Opie bullied, either.

Andy takes Opie fishing and tells the story of when he was once a little boy. He was nearly bullied out of his special fishing hole, Andy says, but he stood up to the bully and got a punch in the stomach as a result. But that was okay, he tells Opie, because the bully learned Andy Taylor wasn't going to back down.

Opie gathers his courage and sets out for school. A few minutes later he's back in the courthouse with Andy, a shiny black eye and a bright smile on his face. He had to take the pain of being punched by a bully, but his victory was worth it.

We may not have to teach our tweenagers to endure blows by bullies, but negative peer pressure is a bullying influence. "Do what we do," peer pressure says, "or you'll be sorry." Being sorry may mean being ridiculed or losing friends. We have to help our children see that the victory is worth the momentary pain.

Changing Roles

It isn't easy to watch our children endure grief from peer pressure, but we have to give them the freedom to stand on their own as they grow older. The amount of time you spend together and the love you share does not have to change now that your child is a tween. What will change are the roles you and your child have played up to this point.

When your child was born, you placed him on a stage and glowed with happiness as an appreciative audience of friends and relatives applauded. When he walked, you stood by his side and held his hands. As he learned and grew, you were there, guiding his hands, training his mind, shaping his life. When the audience grew small and no one else applauded, you and your spouse stomped, whistled and clapped like mad for this kid you loved.

Now he is older, and your child is ready for you to stand in the wings as he faces his public. Your guidance and discipline are still sorely needed because he is unsure of the limits of the stage and he needs your protection. But as he grows, he will find his own way and test his own limits. Your guidance and protection will no longer be needed, but take heart. Your support, love and wisdom will always be appreciated—the child, even when grown, will still need an approving audience.

4

Seeking Adulthood

Gary

> The young think they know everything
> and are confident in their assertions.
> —Aristotle

You've given birth to that child, kissed his toes as you bathed him and hugged him lovingly each time he left home for elementary school. Suddenly he withdraws from your touch, ducks his head when you reach for a kiss and forgets to call the customary "I love you!" as he leaves for school. What happened? The drive for independence has begun.

Tweenagers want to find approval from people other than their parents—namely their peers and other respected adults. The consistent love which parents have provided is suddenly "kid's stuff." In order to show themselves grown up, tweenagers feel they must turn their backs on home. It is often a painful stage for parents, but it does pass. As soon as a tweenager gains his con-

50

fidence and footing in the later teenage years, he will have
the maturity to acknowledge his love for home and family.

James Dobson explains the breaking-away
phenomenon:

> Teenagers are engulfed by a tremendous desire
> to be adults, and they resent anything which implies
> that they are still children. When they are seen with
> "mommy and daddy" on a Friday night, for example,
> their humiliation is almost unbearable. They are not
> really ashamed of their parents; they are embarrassed
> by the adult-baby role that was more appropriate in
> prior years. Though it is difficult for you now, you
> would do well to accept this healthy aspect of growing
> up without becoming defensive about it. Your love
> relationship with your child will be reestablished in a
> few years, though it will never be a parent-child
> phenomenon again. And that's the way God designed
> the process to work. [1]

Tweenagers, though, don't have the hindsight
necessary to understand God's process. They define independence and adulthood in their own and very unique
way.

The Fear of Being a "Mama's Boy"

The greatest fear of a junior high boy is to be known
as a "mama's boy" or a crybaby. Crybabies and mama's
boys aren't accepted. They aren't "cool" in the social set,
and they certainly aren't accepted by other boys who
have established their independence and social status.

Unfortunately for those boys who are sensitive,
physically small, easily embarrassed or shy about leaving
the protection of home, the situation is made worse by
the self-appointed bully who exists in nearly every
tweenage group. What creates a bully? The desire for
social acceptance and status. What makes a shy kid come

back for continued harassment? The same desire for social acceptance and status.

I'll never forget the year Bill was in our middle school department. At twelve years of age, Bill was six feet tall and weighed about 180 pounds. He was a Christian and a very likable boy. But Bill was also an impossible bully. When a smaller boy entered the room, Bill somehow could never resist the urge to walk over and playfully punch the smaller boy in the stomach or slap him hard between the shoulder blades. It was Bill's way of saying, "I'm in charge here. I have power and I want you to know it."

Whenever we held physical activities or athletic games, Bill was extremely difficult to control. His desire to be the king of the mountain led him to outrageous behavior in football, basketball and swimming. He would push, shove, tackle and nearly drown the others— anything it took to establish his superiority in every field. As you can imagine, we were all relieved when Bill entered high school. I think Bill was, too. There he wasn't king of the hill, so he didn't have to constantly assert himself.

The Use of "Colorful Metaphors"

Boys not only feel this competitive drive in physical situations, but in social situations as well. They like to talk big and brag about their exploits, real or imagined. They are particularly prone to include in their language words which would cause a sailor to blush.

Recently a frantic mother came to me. "I'm a basket case," she explained. "My ten-year-old, a Christian who knows better, wrote this!"

She thrust into my hand a note the boy had written to a friend. The mother's trembling hand pointed to an unprintable profanity. How could her son have written something so vulgar?

Profanity is one of the hardest areas for a tweenage boy to control. Middle schoolers curse because they hear adults cursing on television, in the movies and, many times, at home. They curse because they want to feel and act grown up.

Kids with the best intentions try to find ways to interject a little "adult" language into their conversations. James (a strong Christian tween raised in a Christian family) and I were once talking and he used a rather questionable word. "Why, James!" I rebuked him mildly, "What kind of language is that?"

James blushed deeply. "I heard my brother say it and I tried it out on my dad and he didn't say anything."

I knew James's dad would never let something like that pass. "Your dad must not have been listening," I explained. "I'm sure that is not a word he would like for you to be using."

Tweens curse among themselves because it is part of their own special language—a language they don't use at home or at church.

Jeremy was led to the Lord in our department, and I was pretty proud of the progress he had made. His profession of faith was real and he seemed to be trying to grow in the Lord. One day, however, I visited his public school campus and saw him standing with his group of friends. I could hear them cursing, and Jeremy was joining right in. Jeremy was too embarrassed to acknowledge to his friends that he knew me.

Some middle schoolers may curse because they don't know what is proper language and what is not.

After our country-western jamboree and its mud-fight, I was rinsing the mud from the feet of one of our middle school boys. Another boy standing nearby got too close and I accidentally splashed some water on his Reeboks. "Jee-sus Christ!" he yelled.

He gave me a look of blank innocence when I corrected him. "You mean that's wrong?" he queried.

I found it hard to believe that this kid (who had been reared in church) had never heard of "Thou shalt not take the name of the Lord thy God in vain," but it was obvious he had not learned to apply the principle.

Gregory Monaco believes the primary reason why tweens curse is their inability to express themselves:

> Take a long look at the people, especially the youths, who use foul language as a part of their vocabulary. More often than not, you will find they are unable to express their emotions (usually anger) in a constructive, honest way. Perhaps they've been told all deep emotion is wrong, or they might feel that there is too much risk to share feelings honestly. They probably have many emotions within that they don't share with anyone.
>
> Profanity, vulgarity, and foul language in general is a "safe" outlet for emotions stored inside. Verbal violence lets off steam, even commits symbolic acts of aggression, but does it from under cover. You can call someone a blankity blank and he'll never know why you're angry—just that you are. Many of the teens with whom I've worked had such low verbal skills that they substituted repetitive vulgarities for even simple concepts that they wished to communicate.[2]

Lucky for me, I suppose, I didn't get away with cursing in junior high. Once I wrote a profane note to a friend, but my mother found it. I couldn't even get away with cursing on the basketball court. My mother, who was deaf, once watched me closely during a heated exchange at a game. When I got home she lit into me: "Gary Allan Hunt," she scolded, "I saw what you said!"

Independence Through Other "Adult" Activities

Language is not the only "adult" bridge tweenagers

tread upon. They also feel more "adult" when sneaking a beer or smoking cigarettes. Lawrence Kohlberg, professor of education at Harvard University, notes: "Occasionally a psychological preadolescent may take drugs, as he may drink beer or sneak cigarettes. When he does this, he does this as an activity of an exciting forbidden and grown-up variety."[3]

Kids usually start off with cigarettes. Why? Because smoking is the first assertion of "my body is my own and I will do with it as I please." Kids want to belong to the bold group whose devil-may-care attitude reflects the independence and status tweenagers admire. Smoking lends an air of toughness to boys and sophistication to girls. Look at cigarette advertising—the ads are either ultra-macho or ultra-chic. Smoking can also be a symbol of absolute rebellion. Adults warn kids about smoking and parents forbid their children to smoke, so when a child is angry and rebellious he defiantly lights up.

Angie interviewed former U.S. Surgeon General C. Everett Koop and asked what parents could do to discourage their children from smoking. He replied:

> You can point out the fact that smoking is not a habit that you can pick up and discard when you want to. Nicotine is the most addictive drug in our society. The younger you start, the more difficult it is to quit. We have to point out to kids that there are many disadvantages—your breath stinks, you're not attractive to other people, and if you're an athlete you certainly cut down on your stamina. The health benefits of not smoking are tremendous.[4]

If a child never starts to smoke cigarettes, the odds are great that he will never try any drugs. Those who smoke cigarettes find it natural to move up to marijuana; of those who smoke marijuana, nearly 60 percent will go on to try other illicit drugs. If a child never smokes marijuana, the odds are ninety-eight-to-one that he or she will never try any other illegal drug.

How do you keep tweenagers from experimenting with drugs and alcohol? They have heard the horror stories about drugs and alcohol; they know they are hurting their bodies if they use such substances. But it probably wouldn't hurt to make sure young people know the following facts:

- Marijuana smoke has 50 percent more tar than regular tobacco cigarettes.

- Marijuana tar contains 70 percent more benzopyrene, a major cancer-causing chemical.

- Marijuana smoke produces greater cellular changes in the lungs than does tobacco smoke.

- The psychoactive chemicals in marijuana are not water soluble. They accumulate in the system and it takes about one month for all the THC (the chief intoxicant in marijuana) in one joint to leave the body. There is no other drug used or abused by man with such harmful staying power.

- Marijuana isn't manly. Marijuana appears to lower normal testosterone levels in boys. (Testosterone is the major male sex hormone that is responsible for the physical changes that take place during puberty and for normal adult male sexual functioning.) In girls there are also disruptions of normal hormone levels, with possible accumulation of marijuana's chemicals in the ovaries.[5]

Tweens and alcohol is also a deadly combination. Alcohol can make a kid throw up, miss the best part of the party and ruin his new car. Alcohol causes teenagers to vegetate, regurgitate and urinate. It can give a hangover, put a brain to sleep and create a drug addict (some teenagers become alcoholics within six months after taking their first drink). Alcohol can destroy a kid's liver, get him in trouble with the law and hurt his heart. Alcohol can interfere with teens' reproductive systems, wreck their cars and kill their friends—more than 12,000 young Americans are killed each year in auto accidents involving alcohol. Forty thousand more are disfigured. Alcohol can make anyone act like an idiot. It can tear a family apart. It can kill. Sure, alcohol can make a teenager feel like everyone else at a party, but who wants to be like a group that is mindless, bombed, wasted and dumb?[6]

It's sad, but when tweens see their *parents* smoke and drink, they reason that a little bit won't hurt them. They feel good inside when they use drugs and feeling good is precious when feeling insecure is the alternative.

Before I became a Christian I was a heavy drug user. I have my personal experience to share with kids and I can relate to where they are coming from. My kids know that I understand what drugs are like and how they can ruin a life. But, most important, they know that I really care about them. Because I really love them, they don't question my motives for standing against drugs.

It is almost impossible to "preach" a kid out of drug use. It is very difficult for parents to "plead" a kid out of drug use. The best way for parents or youth workers to keep tweenagers away from any drug is to make sure that their tweens are secure enough so they don't need drugs to feel good or grown up.

Tweens in a Material World

You've probably noticed the onslaught of TV programs and advertising aimed at older children. Advertisers, television programmers and movie makers are gearing their pitches toward tweenagers. "People are beginning to realize tweens are a major market," says Selina Guber, a psychologist and president of Children's Market Research, who recently completed a survey of 1,000 kids ages 6-14 and 500 mothers. "In the past six months, I've been getting calls from advertisers around the country. They say they've been overlooking a very important market segment. Not just toys and cereals, but household items: high-tech, video, stereos."[7]

"Tweens are the last frontier for marketers to hawk their wares," says Sheldon Hirsch of Bohbot and Cohn, an ad agency specializing in the youth market.[8]

Another way tweens pursue adulthood is through the trappings of status. How is a parent supposed to keep up with a tween's desire for status symbols? It helps if your child has an allowance for doing chores around the house. Other tweens have babysitting or lawncare jobs. A *YouthTrends* newsletter survey reported that thirteen-year-old boys have average weekly incomes of $22.75; girls that age have weekly incomes of $23.60.[9] That's an annual income of more than $1200, so it is not unreasonable to ask tweens to purchase their own "status" clothing and high-tech gadgets.

Adulthood Equals Privileges

Tweenagers drink and smoke and swear because these are "adult" privileges which they can assume without too much difficulty. Unlike adults, who measure maturity by how one handles responsibility, *tweenagers measure maturity by privileges, granted or taken.* The tremendous drive for independence which begins during the tweenage years is really the desire for the status of adulthood, with all the "privileges" tweenagers covet: the freedom to drive (controlling one's physical surroundings), the freedom from school (controlling one's mental surroundings), the freedom to choose their own friends and circumstances (controlling one's social surroundings).

When your tweenagers are tempted to seek adulthood through unwise behaviors, stress that maturity is not a matter of being able to do what you please, but doing what pleases God, even when the odds are against you. But don't simply pronounce a list of "thou shalt not's." Instead, teach your children the *principles* behind your rules. Teach that true freedom is the ability to choose to do right, not the freedom to do wrong.

Freedom does not automatically arrive at age eighteen or twenty-one when young people can vote, gamble and buy cigarettes and beer. True freedom and maturity arrives when a young person develops character that will withstand the tests of the world.

Through the media and his peers your tweenager is told that grown-up glamour is within his reach. Parents and youth workers must stress that real maturity is also within his reach—it consists of following God's plans and principles.

The Emotional Roller Coaster

Angie

Am I the person who used to wake in the middle
of the night and laugh with the joy of living?
Who worried about the existence of God and
danced with the young ladies till the lark-light?
Who sang *Auld Lang Syne* and howled with senti-
ment, and more than once gazed at the full moon
through a blur of great, romantic tears?
—Logan Pearsall Smith

We were at camp. The speaker had just finished a
stirring and convicting message, and I was counseling a
girl who came down the aisle in tears. "I want to do
better," she sobbed. "I know the Lord wants me to spend
more time in prayer and Bible study, but it's so hard! I'm
going to promise the Lord never to miss a daily quiet time
again."

I prayed with her and secretly hoped she would
honor her commitment. I had seen too many tweenagers

make sudden fervent promises at an emotional moment and fall by the wayside only a few weeks later.

Each Sunday morning and Wednesday night I would ask her how she was doing. "Fine," she would answer, quickly trying to avoid any further questions. A few months later she decided to level with me.

"I've stopped reading my Bible," she admitted. "I feel like my prayers don't go any higher than the ceiling. I wonder if God is there at all. I know I was saved, I remember it clearly, but there are days when God just isn't real to me."

The tweenage years are a sudden merging of childish and adult emotions. Like a cup of cold water thrown on a hot skillet, these emotions burn and sizzle with fierce intensity then die away. Love, hate, devotion, anger, jealousy and happiness burn one minute and vanish the next.

What causes the emotional upheaval of the tweenage years? The child prior to adolescence experienced emotions as a result of *external* activities or objects: a child was unhappy because certain events were bad; he felt love because people gave to him; he felt excitement because an activity was fun. At the onset of adolescence, however, the child begins to experience emotions which have their root in his *internal* being.

These new emotions are bewildering. Girls cannot understand why they feel moody and depressed at the time of their monthly period, and mothers and fathers who question "What's wrong?" don't help. The girls themselves do not know what is wrong.

One Sunday Gary and I crept into church late and sat in a packed pew next to one of our middle school girls. Gary leaned over, caught her eye and murmured a greeting. She lowered her head and began to sob—racking, shaking sobs—with no sound, only tears. I turned to him, bewildered, and asked, "What on earth did you say to her?"

"I said 'hi,' " he answered. "Maybe I scared her."

As we sat in the crowded pew I could feel her small body sobbing through the special music, the announcements and the offertory hymn. During prayer time I scrawled on an envelope and passed it to her: "Honey, is there something wrong? Is there anything I can pray about with you?"

She looked up and shook her head. I looked down the pew—her mother and sister were sitting on the other side and they did nothing but cast clinical glances. They knew what was wrong; apparently our little middle school girl was simply upset from some family fight.

Life has its vicissitudes, but they are magnified during the tweenage years. Joy, pain, sorrow, happiness—tweenagers delight in exploring these new emotions. They will listen to the latest hit record over and over again because the song will either lift them to new heights of joy or plunge them into delicious depths of melancholy. Drugs are often used to experience new highs and lows. Girls devour romance novels to enjoy exciting, vicarious love affairs.

These new emotions are powerful and difficult to control. Anger, rebellion and fear can explode into physical fighting. Fits of anger often result in teary explosions during which time it is impossible to reason with the tweenager. Let the anger subside, then try to sound out the web of emotions and circumstances which caused the outburst. Tweenagers may not know exactly why they feel a certain way, but they want someone wiser and older to understand that they *don't* understand.

Life at the Mercy of Emotions

A tweenager's commitment, whether to home, Christ or an athletic team, may be at the mercy of these ever-changing emotions. Those who work with tweenagers must be sure that commitments are based on *fact,* not feeling. Facts do not change; feelings evaporate rapidly and often without reason.

Several years ago Gary worked with a young man we'll call Chip. Chip's father lived in another state and Chip's relationship with his stepfather was not good. Gary discipled Chip on a regular basis and Chip's growth as a new Christian thrilled us. One night we watched proudly as eighth-grade Chip walked down the aisle and informed the church that he felt called of God to the youth ministry.

Chip then left our department and our contact with him was limited. Gary would occasionally drop him a note or stop by to see him, but Chip's mother was going through another divorce and the household was in turmoil. Chip moved away from home into an apartment with an unsaved young man.

The other night we saw Chip again. His hair was shaved except for a strip down the back of his head—that remaining hair was orange, red and black. He wore a couple of earrings and black leather. He smiled and said hello; we did the same.

When we got home, Gary wrote Chip a letter and gently reminded him of the commitment he made while in the eighth grade. Gary ended with, "If you need anything, please don't hesitate to call," and prayed that Chip would take the time to contact him sometime.

What happened to Chip? What will happen to Chip in the future? We don't know. We only know that his case illustrates a valid point—if a tweenager is given time, love and attention, he can be led in the right way. When he is denied those crucial elements, commitments can be forgotten or forsaken.

Responsibilities are also at the mercy of emotions. Surely you can recall a time in your childhood when you were supposed to clean your room, but a friend came by with a new record and somehow your chore never got done. Or perhaps you were supposed to pick up your brother from school, but you were so upset at failing your math test you walked home in deep gloom, completely forgetting your sibling.

I'm not saying that tweenagers shouldn't have responsibilities—they should. But parents, don't expect your child to have the mental acuity to keep her affairs perfectly in order. She will make mistakes. When she does, have her rectify her mistake and begin again.

Tweenage Worrywarts

Probably the most consistent emotional state in the tweenage years is worry. They worry a lot.

Holly, a sixth-grader, says she worries about "not getting a date." She won't be allowed to date for several years, but she's worrying about it now!

Mike, an eighth-grader, says he worries about "getting rejected by friends and getting laughed at."

Elizabeth says, "I worry about my grades. I get upset when I see a C or a D. I think, *I could have studied more*, or *What a foolish, careless mistake.*"

One boy told researcher Louise Bates Ames, "Most of the time I worry that people won't like me. I worry that I'm going to worry. I worry that I should stop worrying."[1]

Tweens worry about friends, money, family and growing up; they worry about getting decent grades, getting pimples, being fat, being clumsy and being left out. They worry that they will never have a boyfriend or girlfriend, that their freckles are too prevalent, or that their clothes are too old or too outdated. They worry about going to hell, never being able to drive a car and being embarrassed in public.

Boys worry about not making the team. Being part of the team is a status symbol—it means you have worth, that you are good, desirable and a cut above the ordinary. If a boy makes the team he worries about making a mistake, costing the team the game or looking funny as he plays the sport. He feels clumsy, disjointed and awkward. He worries that if he gets hurt he will cry—the embarrassment of crying is worse than the pain of injury. He worries that he will be called "sissy" by the coach or the other players. He worries that his father won't be proud of him or care enough to come to the game.

The boys in our department often play a game we call "murderball." The objective is simple: Get your opponent out by hitting him with a ball. Half the boys are on one side of the gym, the other half is on the other side of the center court line, and three kickballs are given to each team. The balls are thrown at the opposing team. If the ball hits a man, he is out and must retire to the sidelines. If the ball is caught by an opposing man before it bounces, the boy who threw the ball must leave the game.

I was reading an essay by Thomas Cottle and found that he often played murderball (he called the game "bombardment") as an adolescent in the late 1940s. He recalls the worries of an adolescent boy:

> I feared for my face, for my hands and genitals and gut. It was my back and buttocks, I prayed, that would take the punishment. I could not, however, face up to this torture, I mean literally advance head on into this salvo of cruelty and aggression. But I never told a single human being of my fright. Not one single person knew my terror. I simply didn't want to get hurt, but I did feel strongly that if I could just bonk a few guys with that hard rubber ball, maybe even sink one of their lungs when they caught my throw, I'd be in good shape. I would be a better man for it. I would, perhaps, be a man.[2]

Cottle also remembered what it was like to play basketball, "shirts" against "skins":

> Why was it so embarrassing, this exposure of skin and the display of our chests and backs? Some of us had acne and that was humiliating, but I think more

than anything it was that physically we simply were not up to the ideal stature and the ideal posture, size, and strength. The ideal was evidently present in all of our minds.[3]

Girls worry about looking "right." They worry about their clothes and their friends. Girls are jealous when a new girl comes to school: What if the new girl takes away her best friend? What happens if her boyfriend decides to like the new girl? If mother buys daughter a new dress and daughter doesn't know of someone—an "acceptable" someone—who has one just like it or nearly like it, she is hesitant to wear it no matter how pretty or well-made it is.

Girls worry about sports—they hate to be the last one chosen when team captains are choosing teams. They gaze wistfully at the more developed older girls and wish their breasts would hurry and grow. Girls worry about the spurt of growth which causes them to grow taller than the boys their age and stretches their feet longer than they are supposed to be. Girls worry about starting their periods in school or in front of a boy; they worry about wearing a bra or not wearing one because they must undress in front of others for gym class.

Worries at School

More than one middle schooler worries that he will forget his locker combination. Tweenagers worry so much about school that they often experience psychosomatic headaches and upset stomachs. If your child is mysteriously sick before school on several occasions and has no fever, it may be time for a heart-to-heart talk about what worries him.

If your tween has lost his circle of friends from a previous school year, he may be anxious about making new friends. If your daughter has transferred from a small elementary school to a large middle school, she may be petrified at the thought of losing her way between classes and having to endure the humiliation of being tardy. If your son had difficulty in elementary school, he may be overcome with a feeling of hopelessness as he faces subjects like algebra and chemistry.

Since many schools begin tracking, or phasing, in middle school, kids who find themselves in the group of "intelligent" students worry that they will not be able to maintain elevated status. Students with learning disabilities resent the inference that they are sub-normal. They often rationalize their low placement: "School isn't important to me anyway." A student who develops this attitude is likely to carry it with him throughout his educational career.

Worries at Church

Church can also provide occasions for worry. Our middle school department has an organized singing group called "The Light Company." They often travel on weekends and sing in other churches. Occasionally we schedule them to provide the music in our own Sunday school department.

On any other Sunday our kids come into the classroom early so they can meet and talk with their friends. But on Sundays when The Light Company is scheduled to sing, one-fourth of the group purposely arrives late so they won't have to sing in front of their peers. Another fourth will conveniently "forget" to wear their group outfits. Singing in front of strange adults is easy, but singing in front of friends is so embarrassing that our tweens try to avoid it at all costs.

Worries at Home

Church and school provide many opportunities for a tweenager to worry. Unfortunately, a lot of tweenagers worry about their homes as well:

"When my parents fight, I worry that they'll be

getting a divorce and I'll have to choose between them."

"My older sister keeps threatening to kill herself. I feel like I should do something, but I don't know what to do."

"My kid brother gets all the attention. I really don't care anymore, but I used to worry that my parents didn't love me as much as they loved him."

"My parents are always saying 'we can't afford it.' Sometimes I worry we won't be able to pay the bills or that we'll have to move out of our house."

"My dad is always sick, or at least he says he is. I'm worried that he's going to die."

"My mother drinks constantly. I think she's an alcoholic, and I worry that she'll hurt herself someday. She might even hurt somebody else."

"I think my brother is using drugs. His friends don't seem all that great to me, but he likes them better than he likes us. I'm afraid he's going to end up in jail."

Home—the place which should bring welcome relief from the cares of a harsh and demanding world—is often the source of greatest pressure and worry for a tweenager. How about your home? Obviously no family exists without some pressures and difficulties, but when those difficulties come do you resort to worry or to prayerful faith? What is the example you are setting for your children?

Help Your Child Overcome Worry

Try to understand what your child may be feeling when she worries. Assure her that she is not alone: You worried about things when you were a teenager, too. The other girls at school also feel insecure sometimes, even the most popular and beautiful girls. Your tween's key to overcoming worry is to prepare himself for what he must face and accept himself as he is. If your son worries about taking tests, make sure he studies for those tests so he can be prepared. If your daughter worries that her red hair is all "wrong," help her accept her red hair as a gift from God.

James Dobson suggests that tweenagers make a list of their worries, everything that bothers them. This list should be made in private, and nothing should be held back. After making a list, your tween can decide what things can be changed or how he can improve in certain areas. The other things—the things that cannot be changed—must be entrusted to God.

"Commit your life to [God] once more—strengths and weaknesses—good points and bad—asking Him to take what you have and bless it," Dobson tells tweens. "After all, He created the entire universe from nothing, and He can make something beautiful out of your life."[4]

Like a gentle flower which exists for only a short period, this time of budding emotion in your tweenager should be cherished. It is a time of newness, awakening and increasing awareness. Expose your child to the beauty of human emotion, and when difficulties come, lead him by your example.

Rebel With a Cause

Angie

Youth on the prow, and pleasure at the helm.
—Thomas Gray

Dare we suggest it? There is a cloud behind the silver lining of parenthood: rebellion. Full-scale rebellion, not unlike the temper tantrums of a two-year-old, rears its ugly head in the tweenage years.

Although a certain degree of rebellion is natural and to be expected, many parents are caught off guard by the constant battle of wills with their tweenagers. The child who has always been trustworthy may suddenly begin to lie to his parents so he can go along with the peer group he now reveres as his ultimate authority.

In *Parents and Teenagers*, Dr. Grace Ketterman writes:

> The biggest challenge a teenager has is to develop his own personal identity and establish his independence. If not given a chance to break free from the dominance of his parents, at least to a degree, he is

likely to face problems as he becomes interdependent with others during dating, marriage and parenting. Unless teenagers are given a chance to explore and establish their own beliefs, values and behavior while they still have parents to guide them, they tend to turn to their peers for that guidance. I would rather see a teen rebel a little against parents than become overly subservient to the wrong kind of peers.[1]

Why do tweenagers rebel? Aside from the rather inconsequential rebellion which results primarily from "testing" parental standards, rebellion on a more severe scale results from a "broken promise." A study by Arthur L. Stinchcombe[2] showed that adolescents believe certain behaviors should earn certain results.

For instance, good performance in school should result in good grades; good grades should result in parental approval. When the expected chain of events is broken and the unspoken promise is not kept, the adolescent rebels against the "system" and refuses to try again. *If the system doesn't work, he reasons, why should I try? Why should I try my best—which is supposed to get me good grades, which are supposed to guarantee a good college, which is supposed to guarantee a secure job, which is supposed to guarantee a successful future—if the system doesn't work? I tried my best and I didn't get good grades!*

The broken promise can be in any area—family, school, spiritual life. Many times we've had to deal with rebellious tweenagers whose parents have just gone through a divorce: "I tried to be good and make it easier for Mom and Dad, but they split anyway." Other tweenagers may be angry at God for the death of a parent: "God promised to take care of us and He took away my mom."

An adolescent who experiences this total rebellion against the system sees no use in preparing for any sort of future. All that he has been brought up to believe has failed. He can see no use in self-restraint or good performance. All that matters, he reasons, is finding pleasure and happiness for the moment. There is no trustworthy promise for the future.

Dealing With Rebellion

How do you handle rebellion? It is important to realize that severe rebellion is not a sudden action but a gradual process. As your child advances through the years of early adolescence, he learns that he is truly "in between": He is expected to be much more than a child but much less than an adult. He encounters frustrations when he attempts either grown-up or childish behaviors. How he handles those frustrations will determine whether he accepts his position in life or rebels against it.

Communication Is the Key

As you see your child begin to grow toward maturity and independence, make it a priority to keep communication open. Take your son or daughter out to McDonald's for a Coke and a hamburger, and encourage him or her to talk! Shopping won't do it and neither will a movie. Consciously make opportunities to simply have a good talk with your tween.

Find out what bothers your tweenager and discern his reactions to his problems. Discuss how to handle anger, hurt and disappointment. Show him by your example that maturity involves knowing how to handle life's "bumps" without bitterness. Share with him the peace, joy, faith and self-control of the Holy Spirit. If necessary, be ready to explain why a "broken promise" is no reason for quitting in life. Use your wisdom and maturity to help the child learn that the promise was broken due to circumstances beyond his control.

Most of us would never dream of ignoring our mate if he or she came home angry or hurt, but so many parents ignore their children when they are upset! Somehow we get the idea that young people only have small, inconsequential problems, so we don't probe behind the closed door or wonder why Johnny has no appetite at dinner. We think that kids' problems are rather easily solved or forgotten. We find it easier to take the child shopping to "take his mind off it" than to sit down and make a concentrated effort to talk about the problem.

When you talk with your tweenager about his rebellion, be sure to convey the following messages:

1. You've noticed changes in him that have perplexed you. If you have responded incorrectly or ignored the problem, apologize.

2. Adolescence is a period of change, and frustration is built into the tweenage years! Although he is facing pressures unlike the ones you faced, you love him tremendously and will do all you can to help him through these years.

3. He is growing toward maturity and soon he will be on his own with total freedom, responsible only to God. As he grows, his freedom at home will increase more and more, but on a timetable established by you, his parents.

4. He is not grown yet! As much as he'd like to be able to do entirely as he pleases, he cannot have the freedom of an adult while still a tweenager. What he wants is the best of two worlds—the irresponsibility of childhood and the freedom of adulthood.

5. You are responsible to God for his safety, wellbeing and spiritual development. Let your child know that you will try to be more receptive to his feelings and needs, and that you will carefully consider any new requests for privileges. But there will be times when you, as a parent, must say no. When that happens, your child should know that

no amount of whining or pouting will change that
decision. As parents, you will strive to be fair and
firm.[3]

Approach Your Tween Now

Those of us who have worked with tweenagers have
seen kids who, even at this early age, have tremendous
chips on their shoulders which alienate them from our
efforts to reach them. Eddie is one such young man. He's
bright, physically advanced for his age and a leader in his
peer group. But any efforts of ours to engage him in
friendly conversation or simple fun are quietly rebuffed.
He argues simply for the sake of arguing. His countenance is never open or joyous—it is always sullen and
distant.

Gary has talked to Eddie's father, who is unaware
that Eddie has a problem. Either Eddie is adept at hiding
his feelings at home, or his parents simply assume that
his moodiness is a passing phase.

I've seen enough young men and women like Eddie
to know that unless someone probes deep enough to find
out what the broken promise or disappointment is, Eddie
will only grow more and more detached and spiritually
cold. It is possible that someday Eddie will hear a sermon
or learn a spiritual truth that will help him analyze his
own problem, but it is a shame that so many years will
be wasted in indifference and silent rebellion.

If you see that your child has been hurt or disappointed, sit him down for a heart-to-heart talk *immedi-
ately*. Don't allow the problem to fester, thinking, "Oh,
he'll get over it in time." Unresolved hurt encourages the
development of indifference.

If the mask of indifference is already imprinted onto
your child's face and your efforts to talk to him have
failed, I strongly suggest that you find a Christian counselor who will be able to win his confidence and find the
root problem. Your pastor, a respected teacher or youth

pastor may be able to help. Just make sure your child respects the counselor and that the counselor is going to treat your child with the same respect.

Most important, if your tween's rebellion is more than you can handle, be willing to admit that your child has a problem. There is more to rebellion than breaking rules, flaunting authority and screaming at adults. These loud and disruptive behaviors are only symptoms of other underlying problems. Tweenagers generally will not rebel against people they respect, so keep your tween's respect by taking the time to show you care.

Explain the Principles Behind Your Rules

For the rebellion which is really a "testing" of parental authority, talk about your rules, guidelines and standards, and explain *why* you hold these standards. Don't patronize or antagonize your child—remember that he is learning to think for himself. Your reasons for disallowing an activity must be founded on biblical principles. Rules without underlying principles are sure to be broken.

For example: Mr. and Mrs. Jones do not want their daughter to date non-Christian boys. But instead of offering a reason when their daughter questions, "Why not?" they simply respond, "Because we said so. That's reason enough."

Their daughter will adhere to the rule as long as she thinks she may get caught. However, if the occasion arises or if she is away from home, she may happily take up with a young man of whom she knows her parents would not approve. Aside from the objection of her parents, which she has disallowed, she does not see a valid reason why she shouldn't.

Mr. and Mrs. Jones need to explain their principles behind the rule: "We would prefer that you not date non-Christians because every date is a potential mate. We also feel that in order to have a mature and fulfilling relationship you must be able to relate to your boyfriends not only on a mental and social level, but also on a spiritual level." Their daughter would now understand their rule and be more willing to consider their standard as a permanent principle for her life.

I taught twelfth-grade English in a Christian school one year and was surprised to hear that three of my former students had run amuck after graduation. As soon as they were free from the rules of the school (and since they were eighteen, they felt they were free from their parents' rules, too), they spent their nights in bars and nightclubs, wildly seeking what they thought they had been denied. What the rebels were actually lacking was a set of principles they could believe in through all of life's situations. They had heard such principles, I am sure. They simply had never integrated the principles into their own lives. When the rules ended, so did their convictions.

As you talk with your tweenagers, don't just describe rules and the penalties for breaking them. Discuss the principles which support the guidelines. Make sure your tweenager understands your consistent support and the inevitability of your discipline if the guidelines are not followed.

When it comes time to disciplining your tween, maintain honest communication and safeguard his trust. Make sure the circle of confession is only as large as the circle of transgression. Don't make the broken rule and subsequent punishment a matter of public record.

Serious Rebellion in the Tweenage Years

Every tween spells trouble sometimes. But some children, especially in their adolescent years, can turn trouble into a pain-filled way of life for their families. Violence, profanity, crimes, substance abuse, sexual activity, refusing to abide by house rules—such irresponsible acts are in a different league from the usual parental challenges.

"These home-shaking disappointments make you understand why the word rebellion happens to contain the words *rebel* and *lion*," writes R. A. "Buddy" Scott in *Relief for Hurting Parents.* "Living with an out-of-control teenager can be like living with a lion on the rampage!"[4]

I spoke to Scott, who directs a Christian counseling agency in Lake Jackson, Texas, about serious rebellion and how parents can deal with it. "Hurting parents, God understands how you feel," Scott says. "God lost His kids . . . and no one can say He didn't raise them right, either."

What is the difference between "big-time" rebellion and normal adolescent dissension? Scott explains: "There are small indicators and huge indicators. If you look at a mountain range, you can usually see foothills in the foreground and huge, jagged mountains in the background. The 'foothills' are the small indicators—a child's withdrawal from the family, criticism of the traditional values of the family and friendship with kids of lesser moral character. Also included among these foothills would be friends who call and won't give a full name, the rejection of the youth group at church and fudging on curfew. In the foothills, a child is beginning to edge into wrong things, but he does it slowly and keeps his activities hidden.

"In the jagged 'mountains,' though, teenagers don't come home at night, a girl skips school without her parents' knowledge, a boy comes home drunk, a best friend is arrested for dealing drugs. Or a parent finds an incriminating note about sexual involvement or involvement with drugs.

"The typical reaction of parents to tyrannical teens is shock and trauma," says Scott. "They have tried to love their child unconditionally through crisis after crisis, and they ask, 'This is our reward for trying faithfully?' Theirs is a different kind of hurt—it's worse than being fired after you've done your absolute best."

All parents know the feeling of failure we experience when one of our children messes up. But Scott offers comfort. "The misbehaviors of our children do not necessarily indicate we are failures as parents," he says. "As parents we deserve respect. If we are seeking to heal our children and save them from damaging themselves morally, spiritually, emotionally, socially and physically, we are *decent parents.*"

Too often parents react badly when a tween rebels. Scott has seen parents lose their tempers, slap or hit their kids and even curse their children. That approach will not work, Scott cautions.

"Parents should not reject their children in such ways. If you *reject* them, you will *eject* them toward the wrong crowd, and the wrong crowd will be happy to reel them in. We need to reject our kids' wrong behavior but reassure them of our love and trust. Parents have to let their kids know things can get better. They need to maintain their Christian witness. This gives kids a decent environment for improvement."

How should parents discipline tweenagers? Aren't they too old for spanking? And what good is grounding a kid when he has a VCR, telephone, stocked refrigerator and stereophonic sound?

When disciplining, Scott says parents should first decide whether the problem was the result of flagrant rebellion or ordinary teenage antics. "Do not," he says, "make giant hassles of normal teenage problems."

If the problem was normal teenage mischief, be patient. If it was an act of willful wrongdoing, discuss it with your spouse and resolve to respond in unity. "Resolve to be shepherding parents, not vengeful, attacking or punishing," says Scott. Discipline should be done with the desire to teach, says Scott, not to belittle, or obtain revenge, or make your tween miserable.

When deciding what to do, consider what would be

the natural consequence of his or her actions. If it is possible, allow your tween to experience the pain of his wrong choices. But before acting, ask yourself, *Will this heal?* If your response will not heal with time, change it.

Scott suggests that parents speak to their tween and say, "We love you and we know you have good qualities even though you have made a mistake. But because you have chosen to teach us that you can't be trusted (lack self-control, etc.), you have chosen for us to respond by keeping you at home (or by not buying that jacket, etc.). Here's how you can teach us to trust you again in the the future, and here are the positive rewards for your success: (name the conditions and rewards)." Listen to your tween's response.

While the uncomfortable consequences are taking place, be supportive of your tween and remind him that it will be over soon. With such an attitude, parents allow their children to see that discipline is something children bring on themselves, and even though parents have to act, they still love their kids.

"Parents should not leave their children without a Christian parental witness and just give them over to the world. It's very much like the kids are in a life raft and parents are the lifeline. You can't just cut the rope and forsake them. They have to know their parents still love and care for them.

"But there is a point when parents should say, 'I've done my best and now it's up to you. It's time for you to fly out of the nest. You can either fly and soar or fly and fall. If you fly and soar, I'll applaud. If you fly and fall, I'll pick you up if you really want help.' "

Scott believes in the value of family counseling. He has too often seen kids who tearfully return to parents after running away, begging for another chance, and only taking a vacation from their wrongdoing. As soon as they are nursed back to health, the kids are back into their destructive behaviors. The kids are not willing to pay a price for change.

Where can parents go for help? Scott believes that parents should go to any "understanding person who can help them put forth their best attempt to rescue and recover their child." Most important, though, parents should seek help from God.

"Too many parents wonder why God won't answer their prayers and 'fix' their problem," Scott says. "They wonder why God allowed it to happen. They don't realize that an understanding God is with them, and He is loving their child, too. God is not making a miracle to make the problems go away, because He has promised every person free moral agency. He would have to barge into the child's control center and take over to answer many parents' prayers.

"We pray astray when we ask God to do what He won't do. He didn't even barge in when Adam and Eve sinned—He let them exercise their rights as free moral agents. Free moral agency is really important to God, and we often don't understand that."

Church members can help hurting families by supporting and not criticizing, Scott says. "A truly loving church says, 'Even if you've made some mistakes, our position is to love you and support you.' "

Many parents opt to send their destructive teens to residential treatment centers. Scott offers several cautions: "Treatment centers must be investigated thoroughly. Many non-Christian substance-abuse centers, for example, are against their patients using alcohol or drugs. But patients can be profane, smoke, listen to the worst kinds of music, be against parents. And they are taught that sex outside of marriage is okay as long as they are sensitive to the other person's needs. It's often the blind trying to lead the blind and getting paid enormous fees for doing so.

"What should you look for in a treatment center? You want a place that's clean and organized. You want therapists who have their lives and integrity based upon the Rock of Jesus Christ instead of sand. The therapist should be loving and approachable, and someone who can relate to your child on an emotional level. Look for the therapist's credentials and ask about his work experience. Finally, you want a program that has already established a good reputation for helping and healing adolescents."

Newsweek magazine has reported that 43,000 children under eighteen were admitted to private psychiatric hospitals in 1986, compared with only 17,000 in 1980.[5] Is the increase related to a dramatic rise in the problems of teenagers or a tendency for experts to hospitalize teens too quickly?

Scott believes that unless a teenager has evidenced suicidal gestures, dangerous behavioral problems, criminal behavior patterns, or severe drug or alcohol addiction, parents should investigate Christian counseling instead of a treatment center. He calls himself a "life coach" instead of a "counselor," because too often kids think they are somehow "defective" if they have to go to a counselor.[6]

In *Relief for Hurting Parents,* Scott outlines several questions parents should ask a prospective counselor:

- In your counseling, do you honor traditional Christian ideals and values? Are you a Christian?

- What is your stand on premarital sex? Abortion? Smoking pot? Using drugs? Teenagers drinking alcohol? Sixteen- or seventeen-year-olds coming and going without asking permission from their parents?

- Do you follow a counseling approach that holds people responsible for their own attitudes and behaviors?

- If you discover that ours actually is a case where

basically reasonable parents are trying to pull their rebellious teenager away from the wrong crowds and self-destructive behaviors, how will you go about helping us rescue and recover our child?

- How much and how often do you involve the parents in counseling?

- Do you mind if we call you periodically to see how things are going and to receive an updated overview of your treatment plan for our child?[7]

Once a family has confronted their problems and gone through whatever is necessary to recover their tween, how can they be sure their son or daughter does not lapse again? Scott says two things are crucial: a change of mind, and a change of crowd. "I have never," says Scott, "not a single time, seen a kid change and stay changed unless his parents required a complete break with the wrong crowd. In fact, the Bible establishes that 'evil company corrupts good habits' " (1 Corinthians 15:33, NKJ).

"Christian kids are essential to this. If your child goes through counseling or treatment and comes out with a new mind-set and wanting to try his best to succeed, and Christian kids are faithful to him, he will change his crowd and there can be more assurance that his conversion from degenerating to regenerating will be permanent."[8]

Keeping Rebellion to a Minimum

How can a parent bring up a child so that problems with rebellion will be minimal? By teaching through example and attitude the principles of authority.

Each of us has a higher authority. As citizens we are under the authority of the laws of this country; as Christians we are all under the authority of God and His Word.

Parents and youth leaders who show a healthy respect for authority and the rights of others will impart that respect to their children. Parents who attend worship regularly and financially support their church will teach their children to respect God. Most important, parents who respect and apologize to their children and to each other when necessary will illustrate that only God is infallible. We owe our ultimate obedience to Him.

My husband always teases me because I was engaged two times during my teenage years. I couldn't help it—I was (like most girls) young, romantic and totally in love with each of the special young men I was engaged to. Though I only had stars in my eyes, my parents, fortunately, had wisdom in their hearts.

After praying and seeking God's will for my life, my folks flatly forbade me on both occasions to marry the young man to whom I had promised my heart at the time. Though you may be sure I cried, pleaded and rationalized my reasons behind my commitment, in the end I knew I had to abide by the wishes of my parents. I had been brought up with the simple verse, "Children, obey your parents." I felt God would not honor a marriage made against the wishes of my mom and dad.

Waiting for God's best wasn't always easy, but I found it when I met my husband at college. I was twenty-two; he was twenty-nine. Given our age difference, we would never have met in high school, but in His timing God worked His plan in our lives.

So parents, raise your children in the protection of the principle of obedience. The emotional, independent and often rebellious thinking of tweenagers needs that firm foothold. Their obedience and your wise guidance will see them through.

7

Physical Changes

Gary

> My eleven-year-old daughter mopes around the
> house all day waiting for her breasts to grow.
> —Bill Cosby

I was a late bloomer. I didn't shave until I was nearly twenty, never grew hair on my chest until I was a legal adult, and spoke in a falsetto voice until I was well into my teenage years. I was a short, sensitive, redheaded kid who cried easily and was picked on constantly.

One day I decided that I would toughen up and I actively fought back. Coincidentally or not, I began to grow and "Squeaky Hunt" became one of the loudest and most aggressive fighters on the block.

In a typical middle school department you will encounter the complete spectrum of adolescent physical development. Many girls will be rail-thin wispy stalks of childhood; other girls the same age will carry themselves with the assurance of womanly dignity. Among twelve-year-old boys you will find kids with five o'clock shadow and others who are four feet tall with pre-peach fuzz. The range of development is large and those in advanced puberty are as likely to be embarrassed about their growth as those at the slow end of development.

Furthermore, teenagers today are physically maturing faster than we did. James Dobson notes this development:

> Statistical records indicate that our children are growing taller today than in the past, probably resulting from better nutrition, medicine, exercise, rest and recreation. And this more ideal physical environment has apparently caused sexual maturity to occur at younger and younger ages. It is thought that puberty in a particular child is "turned on" when he reaches a certain level of growth; therefore, when environmental circumstances propel him upward at a faster rate, he becomes sexually mature much earlier. For example, in 1850, the average age of menarche (first menstruation) in Norwegian girls was 17.0 years of age; in 1950 it was 13.0. The average age of puberty had dropped four years in that one century. In the United States, the average age of menarche dropped from 14.2 in 1900 to 12.9 in 1950. More recent figures indicate the average has now dropped closer to 12.6 years of age! Thus, the trend toward younger dating and sexual awareness is a result, at least in part, of this physiological mechanism.[1]

As you observe tweenagers, you will notice that girls mature physically at a faster rate than boys. Girls usually begin their menstrual cycles between ages ten and twelve; boys are usually thirteen or fourteen before they begin to show signs of change. Dr. Grace Ketterman discusses boys' development:

> The changes in boys are slower, later and less extreme. They begin to get a little hair on their faces, but it doesn't become heavy for several years. Their

voices lower, which is probably the most noticeable change and often embarrasses them. But the most alarming development that boys encounter is the nocturnal emission. This sign is an evidence that they are beginning to develop the ability to become fathers some day, but many parents don't think to explain to their sons what is taking place.[2]

Sex Education: Why and When

In America, 3,000 adolescents become pregnant each day—one million each year. Four of five are unmarried. More than half get abortions. Two-thirds of America's eleven million teenage boys say they have had sex with a girl. Josh McDowell reports that 91 percent of girls who begin to date at age twelve will have had sex before graduation from high school.[3]

Lots of kids are sexually active these days—everyone knows it. We see teenage mothers on the street, and we hear the statistics. We are bombarded by sexual messages from music, advertising and television. It isn't surprising that today's permissive attitudes have encouraged teenage sex even among Christian young people.

It is important that parents and youth leaders explain the tremendous physical changes that are about to take place in your tweenager's physical body. *Someone* must do it. Parents who are shy about frankly talking about sex may ask a youth leader to talk privately to their child. Tweenagers will learn about sex sooner or later, and it is better for a young person to learn from someone who can explain God's plan. Sex, and talking about sex, is like a piece of sod—beautiful only in its proper place.

Connie Marshner, executive editor of *The Family Protection Report* and a mother of three, has written *Decent Exposure: How to Teach Your Children About Sex* (Wolgemuth & Hyatt, 1988). She believes Christian kids are literally being sent into a war zone, and Christian parents are responsible to educate and fortify their kids. The challenge is not too great nor is the battle too far gone, she says.

"You can succeed as a parent in today's world," Connie says. "Despite living in a culture with values and expectations that work to draw your child into a sexually promiscuous, self-centered lifestyle, you can win the battle. You can create a Christian atmosphere in your home, discuss the sexual part of life openly and honestly, and instill self-discipline in your child. You can be the proud parent of a child who honors God in thought, word and deed. On the promise of 'And my God shall supply all your needs according to his riches in glory in Christ Jesus' (Philippians 4:19, NAS), we can build families that overcome any challenge."[4]

If Christian parents have a general failing, it is their "obliviousness to the threat of the popular culture," Connie told us in a telephone interview. "It militates against Christian family values every step of the way and most parents don't realize it. They think, 'Oh, that music is harmless'; or, 'That movie won't hurt anybody.' But that emphatically is not true. There is a lot of harm. Parents don't realize that a systematic attack is being waged by the world at large against our young people and against Christian values."

Though there is a satanic war against our young people, some kids are winning their battles. What do we know about young people who are *not* sexually active? According to AANCHOR (An Alternative National Curriculum on Responsibility), these kids tend to live with two parents who are interested in them, they have at least a C average in school, they have plans for their futures, they don't date at an early age, their parents have moderately strict discipline and a moderately large number of rules about dating, and they tend to be churchgoers and to take their religion seriously.

Connie became concerned about sex education for

her children when her son Pearse prepared for summer camp. She realized he would be with guys engaging in "guy talk," and she wanted to be sure he had accurate information. She searched bookstores for a guidebook on how to teach kids about sex, and when she couldn't find one, she wrote it herself.

She believes parents should not teach sex education as much as *self*-education. "It's self-control they need, not sex control," she says. "There are three phases of education, and all three go on simultaneously throughout life.

"The first level is factual information about biology and God's Word and our bodies. This should begin when a child is very young. Too many teenagers don't know why premarital sex is against God's Word."

She's right. Authors Clifford and Joyce Penner (*A Gift for All Ages*) say sex education should begin with toilet training as parents give the correct parts of the body. By not putting basic biological education off until it is time for one "big talk," parents teach that what we perceive as sexual aspects of our makeup are a normal and natural part of our being.[5]

In an interview, former Surgeon General Koop gave Angie advice about when to teach sex education:

> As soon as youngsters begin to talk and ask questions, they have a concern and interest in their own anatomy and where babies come from. When they get to be about six, they lose interest in sex until they are about nine. You don't have to worry much about them between six and nine. But when they are nine, they really begin to develop a curiosity and this is the ideal time to teach children.
>
> Teach them before they themselves become involved in adolescence and are very concerned about their own sexuality. At that point you're not teaching the abstract, but something that they are deeply involved with and very embarrassed to talk about.[6]

A good sex education program begins before your

child starts to mature physically. But no matter what you have done in the past, begin to address these issues with your tweenager now.

Questions about sex should be answered truthfully and to the extent that the young person wants to know. "The Talk" should not be a one-time event, but several smaller discussions about physical maturation, physical attraction, dating behavior, etc. Above all, sex should be presented as a natural and God-given gift intended for marriage.

Sex education has to be taught with accompanying moral guidelines.* If sex education is offered without values, the education becomes lessons in sexual techniques. It is like teaching an eleven-year-old how to drive a car: You present the car, explain its parts, tell him there is no experience quite like it, and then hope that he waits until he is sixteen to drive. If he's not given solid reasons to wait, he won't.

We must give our children so much more than biological facts. They need our love and support, they need a values system that governs every area of their lives, not just their sexuality, and they need a strong sense of self-esteem and the knowledge that they were created by a loving God for a particular purpose. Most Christian young people know that premarital sex is wrong, but few can give a scriptural reason.

Many parents hesitate to bring up the discussion of sex because they're embarrassed or afraid that talking about sex will somehow encourage it. The opposite is usually true: Kids who can talk openly with their parents

---

* One of the best books we have seen for junior high and high school boys and girls is *Sex: Desiring the Best* (Here's Life Publishers, 1987) by popular youth speakers Barry St. Clair and Bill Jones. This book along with its companion volumes titled *Dating: Picking (and Being) a Winner* and *Love: Making It Last* present a healthy, respectful view of biblical sexuality in the language of today's young person.

are more likely to delay sexual involvement.

Wayne Rice tells the story of a time he was watching *The Cosby Show* with his family. A commercial asked, "What is sexy?" and proceeded to flash a series of MTV-style images across the screen. "We saw close-up views of lips, hips, tummies, rear ends and satin sheets, and finally the product—a bottle of men's cologne," says Rice.

So Rice turned to his family and asked them, "What is sexy?"

During the next few minutes they discussed what really made a person sexy: gentleness, kindness, love, commitment—and other values not found in the commercial they had just seen.

"Many parents mistakenly believe their only responsibility is to give their kids the obligatory 'sex talk,' in which they explain where babies come from," says Rice. "Granted, parents need to make sure their children have a proper understanding of the human reproductive system. But young adolescents need to know much more. Unfortunately, they learn more about sex from the media—TV, movies and music—than they do from their parents or any other source.

"It's not easy to talk about sex with teenagers. It may feel awkward, out of place, and come across like a lecture. Still, it's essential that it be done, not once, but regularly. Your kids need to know you are willing to talk about sex *anytime* . . . If we want our children to know the truth about sex, then we must take advantage of every opportunity we have to discuss the subject with them, and to challenge the false messages being delivered by the media."[7]

Staying Chaste in an Age of Immorality

Another part of sex education is teaching our children how to remain chaste. "We have to instill in the child's heart a desire to do what is right and the belief that he is capable of doing what is right," says Connie

Marshner. "This involves developing a whole series of virtues: obedience, temperance, patience, modesty, self-control and self-esteem.

"Parents don't often think about the third level of education. We have to give our teenagers practical help to empower them to do what is right. They have to have our help in dating and in knowing what to expect from the opposite sex. Nobody tells them that if a guy invites you up to look at his pictures, maybe that's not what he really has in mind. They need our practical battlefield experience. They need to know what to say when kids hang around and talk about their sexual accomplishments. They need to learn other ways to say no, not just 'because the Bible says it's wrong.' They need to know about the dangers of AIDS and other diseases they can get, and they need to be able to articulate their self-respect."[8]

Connie gives ready and practical answers for the typical lines guys and girls use on each other:

"You don't know how to have any fun."

"Yes, I do; I've had a delightful evening. Let's just leave it that way, shall we?"

"You don't understand. Guys have to have sex."

"Nonsense. Nobody ever died of abstinence before, and you won't be the first."

"I love you so much that I want to give you something more."

"Okay, so give me your self-control, and let me keep what I cherish, control over my own body."

"Don't you love me?"

"Well, frankly, if you're that kind of person, not at all."

"Everybody does it, you know."

"I'm not everybody."

"I'll bet you're just scared."

"Of venereal disease, yes. Of illegitimate pregnancy, you bet."

"But I'll take care of you."

"Thanks, but I can take care of myself for now."

"It's only natural."

"So is death, but I don't want to practice that, either."[9]

Connie's two sons were friends with Toby, a neighborhood boy enrolled in a semester-long seventh-grade sex education class. "Consequently, my boys began asking me questions that I could tell were inspired by Toby's conversation," she says. "Ten-year-old Michael, for instance, strolled into the kitchen one afternoon as I was peeling carrots and casually asked, 'Hey, Mom, what's bisexuality?' I decided they needed some facts to counter the impression Toby was probably giving, so Pearse and I spent a couple of hours during our home-schooling one week to go over the facts of life. After those two hours, Pearse said to me, 'Well, Mom, I think we've just about covered it. How come Toby has to spend a whole semester on it?"[10]

The topic of sex education has been raising the blood pressures of educators and parents for years. The educators see themselves as dispassionate dispensers of information about sex, AIDS and birth control while they preach a message of responsibility. Angry parents often fight for their right to teach their children about sex, but are we really willing to do it?

We must be. In an age when AIDS kills and teenage pregnancy and abortion destroy the innocence of youth and the promise of the future, we must not forfeit our responsibility to our children. The schools will not do the job as we would have it done. They will not teach about Christian responsibility, God's command for purity, or that self-control is a fruit of the Spirit and available to every Christian. Schools will teach about alternative lifestyles, bisexuality, birth control and abortion.

If we are going to teach our children, we must give them more than the sexual "Thou shalt not's." One sixteen-year-old boy sarcastically told *People* magazine, "The only kind of discussion that parents want is one that ends with 'Gee, Mom and Dad, you're so right and I'm not sexually active and won't be at least till I graduate from high school.' "

Christian parents have too often been guilty of simply looking children in the eye and saying, "Premarital sex is a sin. Don't do it!" Now is the time to open our eyes, put away our embarrassment, pull together our courage and begin saying something more.

Teaching Dating's Rules of the Road

We'd like to say up front that we don't think ten-to-fourteen-year-olds should "date." The statistics speak for themselves: The earlier a tween begins to date, the more likely it is that he or she will have premarital sex.

Age of Dating	Percent Who Have Sex Before Graduation
twelve years	91 percent
thirteen years	56 percent
fourteen years	53 percent
fifteen years	40 percent
sixteen years	20 percent[11]

For a more complete discussion of when dating should begin and of dating standards, see our books *Now That He's Asked You Out* and *Now That You've Asked Her Out*, which are designed for tweens and their parents to read together.

Regardless of when a child actually begins to date, boys and girls discover each other in the tweenage years. Years ago tweenage boys were only one step removed from the "cootie" stage, but societal factors have eroded that innocence. Thirteen-year-old girls do become mothers every day in America, and tweenagers talk about sex as openly and frequently as older teenagers.

While we may not allow our tweens to "date," it is helpful for us to teach proper dating behavior for the times when tweens find themselves alone with their special boyfriends or girlfriends.

When I teach I enjoy using an analogy that likens dating to driving. Maybe this analogy will work for you and your tween. If you were like me, you probably did the most intense studying of your life when you were issued a study guide by your state's Department of Motor Vehicles. That thin green paperback was easily the most popular book at my high school. We studied it, memorized it, and finally tossed our copies aside to go in and bravely take the DMV's written driver's test. We all knew how to drive, but we knew the Department of Motor Vehicles wouldn't give us a license if we didn't know things like how many car lengths it would take to come to a full and complete stop at fifty miles an hour.

As parents, we wouldn't let our kids drive unless they knew the rules of the road and were properly licensed. But is your tweenage daughter going out with a boy (though they may not be going anywhere) without knowing dating's "rules of the road"? How prepared are our kids to face "dating traffic"?

Teach your children that *green means go.* The green light doesn't mean, "Step on the gas"; it means, "Proceed if the way is clear." Tell your tween that she will get a green light to begin dating when you feel she is mature and responsible enough to handle whatever might come up. Assure her that waiting is better than beginning to date through dishonesty and sneakiness. People who run red lights eventually get into serious trouble.

Yellow means caution. Although most drivers speed up and rush through yellow caution lights, my driver's manual said yellow means, "Prepare to stop or proceed with caution." Is your tween in a hurry to begin dating? Does he feel pressure to have a girlfriend just because his friends are paired up? Encourage him to be cautious.

Every person has his or her own timetable, and if your tween doesn't want to date, let him know you don't expect him to.

Beginning drivers should know how to drive defensively and make allowances for other drivers. As your tween begins to hang around the opposite sex he should be "defensive," too. Girls need to know that boys are "turned on" by sight; boys need to understand that a girls' revealing dress may not be meant as a come-on. Tweens need to be taught how to dress and act modestly.

Do Not Pass signs are posted whenever driving is risky: on blind curves or narrow mountain roads. Out on the open highway, passing is perfectly legal. But in dangerous situations, drivers risk their lives by disobeying do-not-pass signs.

Tell your children to think of "passing" as affectionate physical contact. Out in the open, surrounded by friends, some light physical contact is perfectly normal between two young people who like each other. Holding hands, an arm around the shoulder—there is a time and place for each of these.

But there are certain risky situations where physical affection should be avoided. If your son finds himself with his girlfriend in a deserted classroom, a darkened hall, a parked car, or an empty house, physical affection can really get out of hand.

Red means STOP! A stop sign or a red light each means, "Come to a full and complete stop." But *where* a driver stops is almost as important as *when* he stops. Lines are drawn on our roads, but there are no "stop lines" in dating. Teenagers often ask, "I know all the way is too far, but where along the way do we stop?"

Teach your children when to put on the brakes. When a couple first get together, they usually hold hands. Next comes a gentle kiss, then later, more passionate kisses. Kissing usually leads to petting, which is a "warm-up" for intercourse.

Clearly explain to your son or daughter that a definite *Caution Light* exists around kissing. For two tweenagers, petting is definitely *past* the stop sign.

When we *Yield* in traffic, we let oncoming traffic pass us by while we wait until the road is clear and safe. It's dangerous to rush out into traffic just because everyone else is forging ahead, and if your child feels like the last virgin on earth, assure him that he will not be sorry for waiting for the one God intends for him to marry. It may seem old-fashioned, but God's plan of abstinence from premarital sex was best even before AIDS, VD and unwanted pregnancies made the news.

A *Slow* sign means just that: "Move slowly!" But too often drivers think, "Aw, I can handle that curve . . . " Then, CRASH!

Remind your tweenager that her future dating years can be a delight and a discovery, but too many young people take dating too fast and end up losing control. They are then faced with the guilt of an abortion, or an unplanned pregnancy, babies, responsibilities and canceled futures. Couples who wreck their dating lives wound their families, each other and themselves.

Drivers who endanger the lives of others often have their licenses suspended. Gently tell your child that if he cannot date responsibly, you may have to "suspend" his license for a while.

Let your tween know that you are always available to help with dating problems. As a parent, you may have excellent experience to share with your tween. Your pastor or youth pastor may be able to counsel your tween. Assure your tween that you and God will always love and forgive mistakes.

Three organizations may be able to help you or your organization with teaching tweens about sex.

SEX EDUCATION RESPECT, INC. provides sex education materials with a Christian slant for public junior and senior high schools. Contact them at: P. O. Box

349, Bradley, IL 60915; (815) 932-8389.

TEEN-AID produces educational materials for parent workshops and senior and junior high curricula. They encourage abstinence, role modeling and strong family ties. Please contact: North 1330 Calispel, Spokane, WA 92201; (509) 328-2080.

JOSH MCDOWELL MINISTRY's "Why Wait?" campaign encourages parents, churches and ministries to teach teens how to resist sexual pressure and presents positive reasons for waiting for sex until marriage. For more information, write or call: P. O. Box 1000, Dallas, TX 75221; (214) 907-1000.

There's No "Shield" From Society

Realistically, I know that not every parent will tell his child what he needs to know about sex. As a youth pastor, I have found that I tread a precarious line between intervening and interfering. "Let the church teach the kids about living godly lives," many parents challenge. But if a child comes to me with questions about sex and I give him answers, I may have an angry phone call later that night: "Some matters belong in the privacy of our home. How dare you teach my son about sex? I'm trying to shield him from it!"

Any parent who believes that children can be "shielded" from sex is not awake in the twentieth century. Practically every sitcom on television explores a sexual theme periodically, if not weekly. At best, they offer the message, "Sex is fine when you're *older* and prepared to be *responsible.*"

Condom advertising is now on television and carried in *Sporting News* and on billboards. Norm Geisler, one of the great intellectuals of our generation and a professor at Dallas Theological Seminary, recently talked with Angie about the movement to advertise birth control devices and encourage young people to have "responsible sex":

> We have 1.1 million teenage pregnancies each
> year and 39 percent of those girls kill their babies. Sixty
> percent of the remaining ones go on welfare. If we
> encourage more people to use birth control, the 10
> percent failure rate which exists across the board will
> automatically be doubled. You will double the number
> of illegitimate births, and the number of abortions, and
> will simply add to the problem instead of solving it.[12]

AIDS has become a household word and is quite
certainly a national threat. Think a moment. If you knew
one pregnant, unmarried teenager in the last five years,
in the next ten years you will probably know a teenager
with AIDS. AIDS is spreading rapidly among those who
practice uninformed, "unsafe" sex—and teenagers are at
high risk.

No, we cannot afford to "shield" our children from
sex education. Nor can we afford to simply let them
absorb the sexual messages which surround them.

Sexuality in the Life of a Tween

A tweenager's social, emotional, spiritual and mental state is profoundly affected by his or her body. Girls
face the greatest sexual temptation in the tweenage years
because they mature faster and are attracted to older
teenage boys. Girls are told that upon menstruation they
will become women. It's a heady feeling to wake up one
morning a "woman" when you were a girl playing with
dolls the day before. A girl's body tells her she is mature.
Her mother suddenly instigates secret and serious
woman-to-woman talks. And her father hesitates to draw
her onto his lap. In her heart, though, a girl misses those
afternoons of quiet and silly girlhood when the world
was uncomplicated. Now she is expected to know how
to kiss, to make a boy like her and to keep a boy interested
at all costs.

Sexual matters are not the first concern of tweenage boys, however. "The boy's world," writes J. M. Tanner of the University of London, "is one where *physical* powers bring prestige as well as success, where the body is very much an instrument of the person."[13] Tweenage boys find that physical prowess either ensures them a high position on the social ladder or condemns them to "shrimp" status. Sexual maturity is not crucial at this age; athletic ability is what counts. The tweenage years can be difficult indeed for boys whose biological clocks are behind their peers'.

When those growth hormones start to flow, though, watch out! Paul D. Meier, author of *Christian Child-Rearing and Personality Development*, describes his fourteenth year:

> I grew ten inches in about fifteen or sixteen months. I was so awkward for a while that relatives quit inviting our family over for dinner—among other things I broke glasses, a camera, and my uncle's pool cue, mostly because I misjudged how long my arms and legs were. And I bumped my head so many times on low overheads that I'm surprised I don't have any residual brain damage![14]

He was lucky. I was so uncoordinated that I fell twice—on two separate occasions—into the deep end of an empty pool. I still have little dents in my head where pebbles were imbedded.

Whenever you wonder if you are going to make it through this tweenage parenting experience, remember what you put your parents through!

Your tweenager may be frightened of these upcoming physical changes. If you don't explain the physical developments before they appear, your child could be scared out of his wits when they arrive. Even if you do explain them thoroughly and completely, your child may still worry about *when* the events will happen, so keep the lines of communication open.

Avoid teasing your tweenager. Let him or her know that physical developments will come in time. Each person is on an individual timetable—that's the way God created us. Physical maturation is a wonderful part of His plan.

8

Mental Mayhem

Gary

A boy's will is the wind's will,
And the thoughts of youth are long, long thoughts.
—Longfellow

I was in the seventh grade and suffering through geometry. Whenever the teacher launched into a lengthy explanation, I launched into my favorite daydream:

There are only two seconds to go in this game and the opposition has the ball. It's a pass—no, wait! Hunt, the rising young star from Ohio, has intercepted the ball! He's dribbling down the court with lightning speed! He's defending himself expertly and the opposition has double-teamed the man! It's an incredible job he's doing, but he's too far down the court to try for a shot. The clock is running out—what? No! Yes! Hunt has just shot what has to be the world's longest goal and it was a perfect swoosh! The Ohio team wins! The applause is deafening. His teammates are carrying young Hunt off the court and into the locker room where the press is waiting. What a star!

Fantasy Island

Practically every tweenage boy and girl have entertained some version of the above daydream. To be a star—that is the unspoken desire of every adolescent. Within each heart is the precious hope that he or she will be the one in a million who rises to fame and fortune as a rock star, a movie star, an athletic wonder or a brilliant television personality.

The children who used to play with dolls and toy trucks have simply moved their fantasies from toys to daydreams. In this silent, secret world and in the privacy of their bedrooms, tweenagers sing into hairbrushes in front of the mirror, shoot paper wads into imaginary basketball hoops, and leap over chairs and trash cans carrying an invisible football over an imaginary goal line. Girls toss their hair teasingly over their shoulders and dreamily kiss the mirror, thinking of the day when it will be real. Boys primp and flex in their underwear.

Imagination is fueled by the exciting prospects of reality—"I *am* growing up! I *can* be a star! I can be whatever I want to be!" Of course the tweenager's emotions often hamper his mental processes and his imagination, but he is moving into a new area. Tweenagers have learned to imagine, reason and question.

What can parents do to help their children through this whirling time of fantasy and daydreams? First and foremost, when your child announces an incredible, unrealistic goal, don't laugh. Or snicker. Or smirk. Or frown.

Just listen.

Often I would catch my four-year-old daughter acting out her fantasies with her dolls. She would be loudly singing and talking in her little-doll voices. If I snuck up and took a peek with one of those proud parental grins on my face, inevitably she would look at me, blush and put her toys away.

A parent's "isn't-that-cute?" expression will kill joy

and imagination. So will a parent's scorn or disbelief.

So when your tweenager comes to you and announces that she would like to be an astronaut, smile and say you wish you had that opportunity when you were growing up.

If your son wants to develop microchips in Silicon Valley (and you don't even know how to turn a computer on), pat him on the shoulder and praise him for his intelligent ideas.

If your son or daughter wants to be a bartender, smile and say, "You have so much talent that you could do a thousand things more challenging." Discourage bad ideas by encouraging good ideas.

We asked our tweenagers what they wanted to do with their lives. Each response was truly individual and ranged from a vague "whatever God wants me to do" to "full-time Christian ministry." Mike wants to become a gourmet chef: "I love to cook. It offers a lot of money, and it requires leadership skills which I feel I have."

Encourage creativity. Most of all, don't forget to pray. The men and women of the future are built from the dreamers of today.

Think Like a Tween

What other things do tweenagers think about? Do they worry about the bomb, or the world population explosion, or the national deficit like we adults? None of the tweens we know do. Of course they may give such issues a passing thought, but most tweenagers are far more worried about their friends, families and school.

"I worry about my friends," says Beth, "and whether they are going to heaven or hell."

A friend of ours is an eighth-grade English teacher and she requires her students to keep daily journals. A recurring theme in the journals is, "I don't have any friends. I'd rather be dead." Tweenagers are not as concerned about global affairs as they are affairs of the heart.

The Age of Reason Dawns
Angie

Mental mayhem is also evidenced by the new reasoning processes which tweenagers begin to develop. Jerome Kagan, an expert on human development, writes:

> The twelve-year-old has acquired a new cognitive competence—the disposition to examine the logic and consistency of his existing beliefs. The emergence of this competence is catalyzed by experiences that confront the adolescent with phenomena and attitudes that are not easily interpreted with his existing ideology. These intrusions nudge the preadolescent to begin an analytic reexamination of his knowledge. [1]

While a seven-year-old finds it difficult to deal with hypothetical situations or situations he knows are not true, tweenagers can more easily grasp situations that they have never before considered. But such imaginings can lead to difficult mental problems.

For instance, suppose we provided children with the following information:

1. All three-legged elephants are red.

2. Sue is carrying a three-legged elephant.

If we then asked, "What color is Sue's elephant?" a tweenager could easily deduce the correct answer. A seven-year-old would most likely refuse to answer because three-legged elephants don't exist and no girl could carry one.

How does this reasoning affect the daily lives of tweenagers? In countless ways. Let's illustrate:

1. God loves man.

2. God creates little babies.

3. Many babies are born disfigured.

4. If God loves man, why does He create disfigured people?

Young people who have always held the first two statements as absolutely valid will be forced to examine them again in the light of the third statement and resulting question. Many tweenagers find that everything they have been taught since birth suddenly has become tentative.

Wise parents and youth leaders have insights to draw upon in their reasoning which the average tweenager does not have. For instance, we know that God does not create disfigurements from spite. We live in a fallen world and many troubles of the world are a direct or indirect result of sin. It is a wise adult who will admit that there are questions and puzzles which are beyond human understanding or reasoning.

Another situation:

1. My parents always know what is best for me.

2. My parents have failed me in some way.

3. If my parents always know what is best, how can they fail me or make a mistake?

Upon examination, most tweenagers will decide that the first statement must be false. Parents do not always know what is best, the child will reason, therefore they can fail, and perhaps their next decision for me will be the wrong one.

"Why can't I date at thirteen?" a girl may ask her parents. "All my friends are dating. I'm responsible and you always tell me I am mature for my age. Don't you trust me?"

"I'm the only one at school who hasn't seen that movie," a boy may challenge. "So what if it's rated R—the people at the theater don't care if I'm under age, and I hear worse language at school every day. Why don't you want me to see *Nightmare on Prom Night, Part 8?*"

Such reexaminations are natural. But because the very nature of such examinations threatens everything parents have been trying to teach the child since birth, many parents are threatened when such questions arise. They try to correct the child's rationale with an authoritarian response: "It's the way it is because I say so!" Such responses only reinforce the child's doubts.

Tweens are particularly alert to inconsistencies in their parents. "You lied!" your son may say, after catching you in a moment of forgetfulness, perhaps after you've forgotten that you said something earlier. "You tell me to tell the truth, and you lie! That's not fair!"

If you are going to tell your tween not to watch R-rated movies, smoke, drink or vegetate in front of the television, be aware that he'll expect you to follow your own principles to the letter. All children have strong senses of justice and fairness, and tweenagers are especially keen on watching for what they see as hypocrisy.

Dealing With "Gray Areas"

"Gray areas" are difficult to explain. Questions which can be settled directly from the Bible are much more simple, but few tweenagers ask simple questions. Their minds constantly ask, "Why not?" Whatever *your* convictions about a gray area, be sure to find a verse which supports your position and share your answers directly from the Bible. Because the world is changing, we must share the unchanging principles of God's Word.

Debbie, a single mother, recently dealt with the gray area of soap operas with her thirteen-year-old daughter Lynn. When Debbie would come in from work she'd notice that Lynn had been squarely in front of the television soap operas since school. Debbie doesn't want Lynn to watch soap operas all day, but Lynn sees nothing wrong with the afternoon entertainment she and her friends enjoy discussing in between classes the next day at school.

"Simply saying, 'Just don't watch them because I don't want you to,' won't work," says Debbie. "That wouldn't have convinced me as a kid, and it won't convince Lynn either."

Debbie searched the Scriptures and then got together with Lynn for a talk. "Lynn, I think you should be aware that everything you see or hear is stored in your subconscious mind," she began. "And the Bible has something to say about what Christians should allow before our eyes and ears." Together they read Psalm 101:2,3: "I will walk within my house in the integrity of my heart. I will set no worthless thing before my eyes" (NAS). Mother and daughter learned the principle *together*, and both have incorporated it into their lives.

You will find that setting guidelines in gray areas is much easier if you find a scriptural principle and discuss it with your questioning tween. If your practice of "seeking and explaining" becomes a regular habit, your child will grow up with the greatest gift you could give him— the ability to use the Word of God for gaining the wisdom, guidance and comfort necessary for a complete life.

And now we have entered an area with room for controversy. There are times when we want our children to take a stand for a principle because *they* believe it. For instance, if my child were offered a marijuana joint, I would hope she would be strong enough to stand on what *she* believes and say, "I will not harm my body. I don't believe in taking drugs," rather than refusing simply because I told her to.

There are other rules and guidelines, however, which are implemented strictly because of my *parental preference*. I may prefer that my twelve-year-old daughter not hold hands with a boy at a "couples only" skate at the local roller rink; however, the situation is not crucial. I doubt if I could convince any twelve-year-old of a biblical principle (other than simple obedience) in support of the rule. Therefore, if I am going to ask my child to conform to such a rule simply because of my parental preference, I need to give my child an answer or some way to "save face" when confronted by her peers.

I vividly remember being the only girl in my seventh grade gym class who did not shave her legs. One day the other girls gathered around me and asked bluntly, "Why don't you shave your legs? Won't your mother let you? Are you still a baby, or what?" If only I had an answer to give! As it was, I was stricken dumb with shame and embarrassment. Fortunately, my mother went out that very afternoon and bought me a razor. She had not intended to let me shave my legs until I was fifteen, but she wisely realized the pressure I faced. Sometimes, you see, a wise parent will re-evaluate her parental preference.

Important and foundational guidelines, however, should be molded into children's lives. A wealthy boy in our youth group planned his birthday party and invited nearly the entire seventh grade of his school. One couple objected to their daughter attending the party. They knew the boy, knew the situation, and were reasonably sure the party would be relatively unsupervised and would involve questionable activities.

Their daughter pleaded and begged, however, and they finally agreed to let her go. "But if you feel uncomfortable with anything happening there," they told her, "call us and we will come and get you."

The girl had been at the party for only ten minutes when she called her parents. The music was loud and vulgar, the kissing games embarrassed her, an R-rated video was playing on the television, and the chaperons were nowhere in sight. Her parents were proud that she wanted to leave, but they were disappointed because she had told the host she wasn't feeling well. Her parents wanted her to stand on her principles, but she simply wasn't strong enough yet to tell the truth and risk the displeasure of her peers.

Spiritual Matters in a Tween's Mind

Tweenagers have questions galore, but they are not deep, probing questions about spiritual matters or theology. In fact we have found that junior high is not the ideal place for in-depth discipleship. Gary used to place a great deal of emphasis on one-on-one discipleship, and he often met on a regular basis with certain boys while other women and I met with girls who wished to be discipled. During our discipleship time we would pray, study Scripture and discuss problems. While these young people were directly involved in discipleship, everything was fine. But after they left middle school and entered high school, they seemingly forgot the deep spiritual truths we so eagerly imparted. Cars, dating and athletics became more important.

Were our hours of discipleship a complete waste of time? No. Whatever they may do, those young people will still remember that we cared enough to regularly spend time with them. They know that we care about their spiritual health, and they know the Bible is the place to turn for answers.

We still disciple kids, but today when Gary picks up a tweenage kid and takes him to McDonald's for a Coke, he is more likely to be discussing sports than sanctification. Gary might ask about friends rather than life goals, and he will challenge the young person to read at least a daily Bible passage instead of memorizing a chapter.

We have learned that the tweenage years are best for building the *foundational* life skills. There is time for God to build the complete house in the high school and college years.

Tweenagers need to learn the basics. If they come from an unchurched home, they need to learn who God is, why Jesus died and how salvation is offered. We teach lessons and relate stories about the men and women of the Bible. Most important, we stress a daily devotional habit, a prayer list and Scripture memorization.

Tweenagers from Christian homes need to learn the principles involved in choosing friends, building relationships with parents and other people, making decisions and maintaining a walk in Christ.

I believe it is very important for young people from Christian homes to have an opportunity for evangelism. Too many of our churched young people are sheltered in Christian schools and so involved in church programs that they never have the opportunity to stand for Christ in the world. Many Christian school children do not even know an unsaved person.

How can you get tweenagers excited about evangelism? It's not easy, but the one thing that will get a kid excited about leading his friends to Christ is leading a friend to Christ. Once they've done it, they want everyone to go to heaven!

To be honest, kids are not very effective at door-to-door visitation unless they are visiting their friends and have a youth pastor or other adult along. The kids usually treat visitation as more of a monotonous chore than an exciting opportunity.

We've found the best way to get a kid excited about leading someone to Christ is to encourage him or her to concentrate on one or two unsaved friends. They can invite him to Sunday school or other church functions, make him feel welcome, and pray for him consistently until he makes a decision for Christ. This one-on-one "friendship" evangelism is very effective with tweenagers. Once one friend is led to the Lord, you've got an excited tweenager on your hands!

Give your tweens the chance to be a witness and a testimony for the Lord. The salt of the world does no good if it is left in the salt shaker. Tweenagers need to practice standing alone in their faith. Let them practice now while a loving home is standing by to catch them if they stumble.

The tweenage years truly set the foundation for the complete mental processes of later years. During this time tweenagers learn to reason and to accept, to question and to have faith, to love and to lead. Though these months are bewildering to parents and tweenagers alike, if communication remains open and parents and leaders are willing to carefully guide the random thoughts of tweenagers, the foundation that is established will be a strong one.

What if Church Is "Boring"?

"My child doesn't want to go to church with us anymore," more than one parent has told me. "He says the services are boring. Sometimes I think I should require him to go to church, but I don't want to turn him off to spiritual things by demanding church attendance. What do I do?"

If you're in a good church where the youth departments are exciting and active, it's very likely that your tween wants to go to church more often than you want to take him. But some kids balk at attending church with their families.

James Dobson has given good advice in this area:

> Though it's wise to adopt a softer approach to spiritual training as a child moves through adolescence, it is *still* appropriate for parents to establish and enforce a Christian standard of behavior in the home. This means that I would require my seventeen-year-old to attend church with the family. But this is one of those points at which effective, sensitive parenting becomes a delicate act. The way he perceives your reasons for imposing this rule will make all the difference in the world. Let him know that, as far as you're concerned, it has more to do with your own

integrity and responsibility before God than with his personal faith—or lack of it.

Tell him, "As long as you are under this roof, we will worship God together as a family. I can't control what you think. That's your business. But I have promised the Lord that we will honor Him in this home."[2]

I agree with Dr. Dobson, and would like to suggest another option for parents with reluctant tweenagers. "As long as we're a family we will attend one worship service together on the Lord's Day," a parent could say. "And then you may choose (at least) one other Christian youth activity during the week."

I really believe parents do their children a great service by finding a Bible-believing church with an active, evangelistic youth department. If this is not possible, however, there are bound to be other options. Perhaps another church has a good youth program on Wednesday nights that your tween would enjoy attending. You may find good programs from Campus Life, the Fellowship of Christian Athletes, Youth for Christ, Young Life or Campus Crusade for Christ—look around your community and see what options are available for your tweenager. Thousands of Christian youth workers have invested their lives to make sure the gospel is relevant and exciting for as many tweenagers as possible, and that includes *yours*.

The Troubled Tween

Gary

No wise man ever wished to be younger.
—Jonathan Swift

Occasionally you will meet a tweenager who is, by the age of eleven or twelve, already a hardened reprobate. Walter is such a young man.

From the first moment I met him, he was hostile, rude and belligerent. He lived in a rough neighborhood, and violence and hatred were a normal part of his behavior.

He came to church only because he wanted desperately to play football on our middle school team. The public school coach wouldn't allow Walter on the school team; we took him because we thought perhaps he would accept the gospel. Walter was in such a state we thought surely anything would help him!

It is hard to believe that a ministry to children this young could already be a "salvage" ministry. Sadly, Walter was too far gone to be helped by our program. He alternately needed and hated us; one week he would seem to be on his best behavior (which for Walter was a sullen stare instead of a belligerent remark), but the next week he would pull something so unmanageable that we would ask him not to return. Throughout his time with us, Walter consistently rejected the gospel.

After being asked to leave each week, inevitably Walter would telephone the next week and beg to come back. We would relent, he would come back, and we would once again find ourselves regretting the decision. The last Sunday I saw Walter he was disturbing the lesson in Sunday school and a worker asked him to leave the classroom. As Al, our volunteer worker, escorted Walter from the classroom, Walter pulled a knife on Al and threatened him. Al once again asked Walter not to come back.

Tweens Face a Different World

You can see the lights going out. It seems to happen somewhere in junior high. A child goes in soft and comes out hard. He enters laughing and innocent . . . he leaves unsmiling and jaded. The eclipse shouldn't some so fast, so soon. But it does.

The moral crossroads that used to come in college or high school have moved to junior high, to middle school. By eighth grade, a young person will probably have to decide about his first drink, his first drugs, his first sexual experience. One out of five will have sex before they enter high school.[1]

The world our tweens face is not the same world we faced in our junior high years. And they know it. Any time you say, "When I was your age . . . " a tweenager will smirk and turn aside.

My parents grew up in a different world than I did. Two generations ago, according to Urie Bronfenbrenner,

Everybody in the neighborhood minded your business. If you walked on the railroad trestle, the phone would ring at your house and your parents would know what you had done before you got back home. People on the street would tell you to button your jacket, and ask why you were not in church last Sunday. Sometimes you liked it and sometimes you didn't—but at least people *cared.*[2]

I grew up in the 1960s, a time of societal upheaval, accelerated technology, civil rights, prosperity, Woodstock, Vietnam, campus unrest, *Father Knows Best,* and an outpouring of drugs and mind-altering substances. I wanted to try everything, and I was convinced my parents were so "out of it" that they couldn't possibly understand all that life made available to me.

Today's adolescent faces all of the above and more. In his world he is bombarded by the media, threatened by nuclear annihilation, encouraged to be sexually irresponsible, and allowed unprecedented freedom from adult supervision.

Sex is the message, the medium and the purported meaning of life. "The pill," says Norman Geisler, professor at Dallas Theological Seminary, "said, 'You can do it safely.' The bomb said, 'You had better do it now because you might not be alive tomorrow.' AIDS is saying, 'You'd better not do it because it might kill you.' School-based clinics which distribute condoms to students are saying, 'We know you're going to do it, so just do it safely and responsibly.' "[3]

The unchangeable standards of my childhood—the home, a moral society, the security of a protective father and a nurturing mother—no longer exist to support today's young people.

Society May Be Killing Our Tweens

Television calls them the wonder years, but for millions of youths between the ages of ten and fifteen, the years of early adolescence are anything but wonderful. No longer children, not quite adults, they are bombarded by dizzying physical changes, reeling emotions and raging hormones. Today's youngsters, however, face problems far more formidable than acne or gangly limbs. Drinking, drug abuse, sexually transmitted diseases and teenage pregnancy, once the province of high schools, have drifted into the lower grades. Add to this the crippling effects of broken homes and ill-equipped parents, and it is easy to see why nearly seven million children ages ten to seventeen are considered "at risk" of becoming troubled, unproductive, even dangerous adults.[4]

How threatening are these changes in society? Very. The only age group in our society with an *increasing* death rate is teenagers. Death rates from disease among young people have dropped dramatically, but death rates due to individual behavior have increased. From 1960 to 1980 motor vehicle deaths increased 42 percent. Suicide among the young during that same time period increased 139 percent. Homicide—young people killing other young people—increased 232 percent.[5]

Today's young people are silently crying out for help. They need to know that they have great worth, that they can find a purpose in life, and that Mom, Dad and others really care about them. Professor Urie Bronfenbrenner has studied child development for years. As a world authority, he knows what tweenagers need: "I see in my studies of children one essential prerequisite for healthy human development and that is *someone* has to be crazy about the kid."[6]

Tweens and Divorce

Divorce is not easy to endure at any age, but it's particularly hard during the tumultuous tweenage years. Kids who are striving to find their own identity find themselves torn between two parents and two homes. It is a difficult, frustrating time.

Living with a stepparent brings further adjustments. Listen to what these tweens had to say about their stepparents:

> I don't live with my stepmom, but I see her every Saturday. She is so nice to me! She never yells at me or anything. Maybe if I lived with her she would be different, but I don't, so I think my stepmom is the greatest in the world.
>
> Melody, age eleven

> The biggest challenge is remembering that my stepfather is not trying to take my real dad's place. Although my stepdad is like a real father, I still love both of my fathers the same.
>
> Guy, age thirteen

> I don't like my stepfather at all. He treats me and my older brother like dirt and treats his real kids wonderful. It makes me sick.
>
> Cassie, age twelve

> I would tell a stepparent to love their stepchild like their own and realize that we go through many frustrating decisions. We try to please them *and* our real parents. We may get upset and say untrue statements about them, but they should just love us and ignore the untrue statements because we appreciate them providing for us.
>
> Nicole, age eleven

> Living in a stepfamily is frustrating because I have a big problem calling my stepmom "Mom." It's also frustrating because my dad always seems to stick up for her, not me.
>
> Michelle, age thirteen

> When you live with a stepparent who cares, it's really encouraging. If you have a real parent who

doesn't care, it really makes you feel good that someone is there. My stepdad is like my real father, and I
love him.

Jennifer, age fourteen

My family's greatest challenge is getting along.
My stepdad gets angry easily and doesn't have much
patience. He's working on it. He hasn't had any kids
of his own, so he probably doesn't really understand
everything. The last few nights he's been doing pretty
good—he hasn't yelled or gotten angry. My mom and
sister went out, and he and I were by ourselves. It was
fun.

Jon, age twelve

The frustrating thing about a stepparent is seeing
this person and no matter how much they try to be
your parent, you don't see them as a parent. I see my
stepmom as sort of a stranger, and that is hard because
I really try not to, but I can't help it.

Michael, age thirteen

Just like any other parent, my stepdad loves, yells
and punishes me, and I love him just the same.

Elaine, age thirteen

Stepparents need to remember that there are times
when a tween would give *anyone* grief. Many times stepparents read ordinary tweenage self-centeredness as personal animosity. Johnny may resent his stepparent, he
may be angry at his parents for the marriage breakup, and
he may blame himself for his troubles. These are serious
problems, and they need to be talked over and handled
correctly by the parents and/or a counselor. But ordinary
tweenage troubles are stirred into the mix, too, and
parents shouldn't overreact.[7]

Tweens and Suicide

A few years ago an outstanding high school junior was killed in a car accident. The community and the family mourned, but no one seemed to give more than perfunctory attention to the boy's younger brother, then fourteen.

Time passed. The younger boy began sitting alone in the cemetery next to his brother's grave. He moved into his brother's bedroom and literally tried to assume the older brother's role. His youth pastor was unaware of these happenings—he only thought the boy was shy or withdrawn.

The parents were bewildered but simply thought, "He'll grow out of it. He's only trying to cope in the best way he knows how."

On the two-year anniversary of the older brother's death, the younger brother donned his brother's varsity jacket and started up the car in the family garage. He was found dead the next morning.

Teenage suicide is not as extreme as you may think. Virtually all tweenagers, whether or not they would act upon their thoughts, *do* think about killing themselves at some time. Christian young people are as prone to this temptation as are non-Christian young people.

The other night our middle school service featured testimonies from the group. Anyone who wished to come up and address the group could. At first no one would budge and there was a general uneasiness and shuffling throughout the room. Finally one girl stood up and began to share what Christ and friends had meant in her life.

We hadn't intended it to work this way, but suddenly the theme of the evening became suicide. One boy stood up and shared that he had found his best friend dead after suicide. Another girl explained that she had attempted suicide and failed. Several kids shared that they had seriously considered suicide, but their friends had managed to talk them out of it.

The other youth leaders and I were amazed. Suicide, or attempts of suicide, seemed to be almost a fad: "If life gets too rough and you'd like to get back at your family or your friends who have hurt you, kill yourself." Somehow our tweenagers had picked up this message, and the thing which stopped them from destroying themselves was *their friends.*

One of our leaders stood and shared that Jesus could be there even when friends couldn't, but Angie and I learned something important that night: To our tweenagers, having Jesus wasn't as important as having a living, breathing, caring friend nearby. That may sound blasphemous, but it accurately reflects the way tweenagers think. They are extremely friend-oriented, and there is no one more miserable than a tweenager with no friends.

Parents, in their own way, can be friends with their tweens. Though they certainly will never replace the need for peer friendships, parents are very important to tweenagers. Dr. R. John Kinkel, who reported to the American Psychiatric Association that nearly eight of 100 U. S. teenagers attempted suicide within the past year, says that young people who have a "solid, quality relationship" with their parents are not as likely to attempt suicide as those who "have weekly blowups with their parents."[8]

Parents, he says, should watch if their adolescent child shows signs of extreme pessimism with "an unnatural tendency to look for doomsday." Teenagers who indicate that it is unlikely they will remain married to one person or ever have children are suicidally pessimistic.[9]

Washington, D.C., psychiatrist Willie Hamlin says parents who provide little personal attention contribute to teenage suicide: "Parents sometimes are so busy working hard to provide the material things that they've neglected what the child really needs and wants—time, attention, love and affection. The child acts out with suicide attempts to get attention."[10]

Why Suicide?

Why do tweenagers, with their "insignificant" problems of friends and loneliness, resort to such a drastic action as suicide? Fran Arrick, in *Tunnel Vision*, explains how young people think:

> Tunnel vision is the inability to see anything else in life but the loneliness and pain of that particular moment. It's the inability to step back and know that things will get better. Grown-ups know that you get over certain disappointments and setbacks, that they won't affect the rest of your life. But kids think, "I wasn't invited to a party," or "I'm breaking up with my boyfriend," and they can't see beyond that.[11]

One teenager put it this way: "It sounds crazy, but I think it's true—kids end up committing suicide to get out of their finals."[12]

Psychologist Iris Bolton of The Link Counseling Center in Atlanta feels that there are four things parents and teachers should teach their children in order to combat "tunnel vision":

> We've got to develop an individual's self-esteem so that each person has an internalized, intrinsic value because of who he or she is, not because of what he or she does. We've got to teach communication skills so that each person can learn to express and discuss their feelings. And we've got to teach what I call "positive failure." In a culture that promotes being "number one" in all that we do, it's important for kids to know that the effort is positive, that they can enjoy and grow from what they do regardless of the outcome. And finally we've got to help individuals learn how to handle grief. Many suicides are triggered by some sort of loss—a parent, a good grade, even a date—we've got to help people learn how to deal with losses and even grow from them.[13]

Helping a Troubled Tween

How can you help a troubled and possibly suicidal tweenager?

Be alert to the warning signs. Suicide threats, personality changes, depression, drop in school performance, themes of death in music, artwork, or school compositions, loss of friends, drug and/or alcohol abuse, and giving away prized possessions are all signs of a troubled person.

Talk to the tweenager. Let him know you're concerned about his well-being and the changes you've seen in him. Offer to pray with and/or for him. Don't be drawn into a debate about whether suicide is right or wrong.

Don't beat around the bush. Ask if he has a suicide plan and try to get the how, when, where and why.

Don't act shocked at what the tweenager will tell you. If there is an underlying reason why the tweenager is trying to escape life (e.g., incest, rape, abuse), report the incident to the proper authorities.

Refer the tweenager to a professional for help. Call the pastor, a counselor, the parents, a psychologist.

Remove any potential weapons from the house. Don't leave a tweenager alone if you believe the threat of suicide is immediate.

NEVER assume the tweenager is "only bluffing."

The tragedy of tweenage suicide hits fifteen families every day, and Christian families are not immune. One week a Christian school student in our town killed himself, and the following week another boy attempted to imitate the act. And it is not only older teenagers who are killing themselves—at least 3 percent of all reported suicides between the ages of ten and twenty-four were between the ages of ten and fourteen.[14]

The need for parents and other adults to be loving friends to tweenagers has never been greater. We cannot ignore them—the cost is too great.

How to Make a Tweenager Your Friend

Gary

By friendship you mean the greatest love,
the greatest usefulness, the most open
communication, the noblest sufferings,
the severest truth, the heartiest counsel,
and the greatest union of minds of which
brave men and women are capable.
—Jeremy Taylor

It is a pity that most young people think adults are incapable of understanding, and most adults think young people are foolish and trivial. "The conversation of the old and the young," said Samuel Johnson, "ends generally with contempt or pity on either side."

You cannot have an influence for good in a young person's life unless you have his respect. You cannot direct and mold his life until you have his friendship.

How can you cross the cultural and social "generation gap" to reach a tweenager? Must you dress like them, think like them and give up a measure of your hard-won maturity in order to relate to them?

No. In fact, adults who try to act or dress like kids usually earn only contempt. Young people want to see adults who act like adults. They want to see a hero, someone they can strive to be like. Tweens need the assurance that it is possible to grow up and be happy and well-adjusted.

It Starts With Involvement

So how do you reach tweenagers—yours or someone else's? First of all, you must be seen by kids. You must be available. This is a foundational requirement for anyone who truly wishes to positively touch the lives of young people.

Go to their activities consistently; attend the school's athletic events and band concerts. Introduce yourself to the principal of the school and meet your kids' favorite (and least favorite!) teachers. When your kids are ranting and raving about Mr. Miller the science teacher, you should know who Mr. Miller is.

What does this accomplish? The kids learn to recognize your face—they know who you are. If you work with tweenagers at church, for instance, showing up at a school event will pleasantly surprise them and show them that your commitment to them is more than a once-a-week exercise. They know an adult is not likely to attend a school function unless he or she really cares.

Parents, although Johnny or Jenny may blush to see you bragging about them, and though they probably won't want to walk into the school with you, your children will be glad to know you are there for their activities. I've heard so many adults with unhappy childhoods say, "There was never anyone there for me. No one cared enough."

Always be there when they need you, but youth workers, take care to be used, not abused. I had always taken pride in my availability, but when some of the girls from church began to call me for a ride to the mall so they could walk around for an hour or two, I realized I had become a glorified taxi service.

The telephone can also be abused. Tweenage girls love to talk and share their secrets, and if they can't get in touch with their best friends, they'll call anyone who will listen to them. Many girls, lonely for someone to talk to, began to call me and talk for an hour or two each night.

I didn't mind at first, but when I realized how my wife resented the way those phone calls cut into our family time together, I stopped the phone calls. "If it is an emergency or if you need to ask a simple question, fine—call me," I told my kids. "But if you just want to talk, please come by and see me at the office or call me there." I let them know I was available *if they really needed me*. I'll never have an unlisted phone number, but I guard my family time at home by limiting my availability.

If you are a lay worker, with a family and a career of your own, you can't be available to attend every function of your city's middle school, of course. But if you can be faithful to your church's middle school activities and be willing to spend some telephone time with a tweenager who needs it, you'll be providing an invaluable service.

And parents, never limit your availability to your children. I know of exceptionally successful men who spend hours working in high-powered offices whose doors are always open to their children. Your child needs to know that you are always there and are willing to hear what they have to say.

Become a Part of the Middle School World

I realize not every lay person or parent can do *all* of the things which I am suggesting, but youth pastors, perhaps you should consider becoming a part of the middle school world. One year I concentrated my efforts on Linkhorne Middle School, a public school in our town, and was permitted to help the football coach with the team. I was strictly a volunteer (any coach can use an extra pair of hands) and soon I had many regular responsibilities. The boys on the team grew to know and trust me, and even those who had never attended our church found out that I was "okay."

Coaching Little League was another inroad to the youth of our city. I chose to coach in the minor league (ten- to twelve-year-olds) and soon found that all my areas of involvement were overlapping—Little League boys showed up in football practice at Linkhorne and eventually turned up in our Sunday school class.

In all areas, I tried to maintain a strong Christian testimony. I often counseled the boys privately. I was delighted when the head coach began to send boys to me: "This boy is starting to get into drugs, I'm afraid. Gary, you have a talk with him."

It wasn't long before I was helping coach tennis, track and basketball at the public school. The school teachers and coaches were glad for the extra help; I was thrilled that I was meeting so many new kids. Slowly and surely I was becoming a regular fixture in the world of those middle school kids.

Perhaps the most meaningful plaque I've ever received was presented to me at the close of the school year. On "Fun Day," when the school held their awards ceremony, I was presented with two plaques for my help. When I saw the glowing faces of the boys I had worked with, I knew the long hours under a hot sun were all worthwhile.

Parents, when your child registers at the area middle

school, make an appointment with the principal and let him know you are concerned about your child. Attend PTA meetings. Schedule conferences with your child's teachers when there is *not* a problem with his grades or his attitude.

Get out there and be known! Don't sit in your little church "bubble," isolated and insulated from the world. The world of tweenage kids is often shocking, irreverent and perhaps not the antiseptic Christian world you enjoy. But you will never be more than a glorified chaperon or an uninformed parent unless you are willing to get out there and get involved for the sake of kids. Never miss an opportunity to expand your base of contacts.

After kids see you around and they learn who and what you are, many will come to talk and "check you out." Here is where a sense of humor comes in handy. Let kids know you are fun and have fun with them! Be relaxed and be yourself. As you get to know kids, those who need someone special may seek you out and you can counsel them and invite them to church.

What Tweens Need From You

And what do tweenagers want from their parents and other adults? Elizabeth, a tweenager, says that she wants a relationship "where my parents can believe me and trust me. Without trust I wouldn't have any privileges. I love my parents, and I want to keep it that way."

Michael says, "I want my parents to give me freedom and to understand me." A tall order, isn't it?

The Friendship Factor

Jim Zug is a Christian science teacher in a public middle school. He's popular, yet firm, and several kids hang around his classroom after school. Why? Because he is their friend.

Jim's "secrets" are simple: "I get to know their names quickly. They know that you really know who they are if you simply remember their name. When I'm with them I talk *to* them, not *at* them. When we talk, we don't talk about school or science or the latest exam. We talk about things they care about."

Greg Wheeler is another popular teacher. "I try to be a friend to them and keep their respect," he says. "I find out what they're interested in and always ask about it: 'How did you do in your game last week?' Kids like to talk about *their* activities, not yours."

Jane Randlett, a lay worker, a terrific mother and the mother of a tweenager, believes it is important for the friendship between child and parent to begin in the childhood years: "It involves doing what they want to do and spending time in their activities. The friendship involves listening, having fun and being together."

When you take your child out to spend time with him, do you drag him to your adult activities or do you let your child choose the activity? Tom, a busy father with a demanding job, always prided himself on the hours he and his son spent together. The twelve-year-old son, however, recently began to pull away from his father—he doesn't want to be with Tom. Why? Because Tom had taken him to adult meetings, adult games, adult events. The boy had never been a participant in their time together; he had only been a token tribute to Tom's fatherhood.

Sharing Christ With Your Tween

After you have established a friendship and you have taken the time to really know that tweenager, share Christ with him. Sharing the gospel *before* you have taken the time to get to know a tween may turn him off. "Preaching" at kids doesn't show you care; it implies that you are speaking out of obligation. Why should a tweenager trust that what you are offering is right for him if you haven't taken the time to get to know him or his problems? Sharing the gospel with a kid who is your friend shows that you care enough to discern his needs and provide the right answer.

When you have been seen by kids and known by kids, it follows that you will be understood by kids. When tweens understand you and what you are about, and when they can trust you and know that you honestly want to help them, then they will be willing to accept the gospel you present. Kids have no problem realizing they sin—they have clear-cut ideas of what is right and wrong. But due to the negative self-image which many possess, they may have a problem believing that Christ loves them enough to die for them. But if a tweenager can look at you and see God loving him through you, he can believe.

Making Contacts With Non-Christian Kids

How can you contact non-Christian kids? First, get your Christian tweenagers to bring their unsaved friends to church activities, Sunday school, or by your office or home for a visit. One of my dedicated Christian boys, Tommy, was concerned about his friend, Steve. "You bring Steve by my office," I told him. "We'll have a couple of Cokes and I'll talk to him." Tommy assured Steve that I was okay, and they stopped by. After spending some time in idle chatter and getting to know one another, I was able to share the gospel with Steve.

You can also contact kids casually by playing sports or other recreational activities. Our YMCA has "open gym" each afternoon and during the summer I try to play basketball every day. I meet many new adults from the community and many teenagers down on the basketball court. We learn respect for each other on the playing field, and once again I've made new contacts.

Church-sponsored activities are also great for making contacts. Once each year our church invites all junior and senior high students to "join us on the bus" as we travel to Kings' Dominion, an amusement park three hours away. Kids come by the thousands and we let them spend all day in the park. After a day of fun and freedom, they meet on the bus to go home, and we present a short gospel message. Many kids accept the Lord on the bus.

Other effective contacts include home visitation, phone calls "just to say hello" and written contacts. Our Sunday school department routinely sends a birthday card to each member, and I've found that kids love receiving a note in the mail. My notes are always short, but whether I simply ask, "How are you doing?" or tell them that I have been praying for them, kids always let me know how much they appreciate my letters. Nothing encourages a tweenager more than an adult's letter saying "thanks" for something nice they have done for someone or complimenting them on their kindness, courtesy, concern, spiritual growth or consistency.

It is helpful for youth leaders to write to parents, too. In today's society, where sexual perverts lure children in hundreds of neighborhoods and gun-toting snipers lurk in parking lots, I understand why many parents initially mistrust me. You see, tweenagers go home and talk about admired adults, and many parents do not know what to make of the influence of a youth pastor. I've found it is important to meet parents, explain that I am trying to help their child grow spiritually, and that I will never attempt to undermine their parental authority.

I've met parents, Christian and non-Christian, who could care less about where their children are going or with whom. I've also met parents who truly resented any outsider's influence on their child. Then again, I've met parents who are thrilled beyond measure that someone cares enough to listen to their child.

We have seen success stories of tweenagers who accepted the Lord and eventually led their entire families to receive the gospel and become part of a church. Those testimonies, and the record of answered prayers in my prayer journal, keep us going.

Do You Remember
When You Were Thirteen?

I suppose I have a special concern for very young teenagers because I remember myself in junior high—skinny, high-voiced, sensitive, shy and terribly insecure.

I remember my eighth-grade Christmas choir concert. I had been chosen to step out between songs and announce the name of the next number. I was nervous, but more than that, I was profoundly embarrassed because hundreds of eyes would be centered on me and me alone. After the opening song, those eyes turned to me. I stepped out on cue, took a deep breath and fainted. Whack! My chin hit the edge of the risers and I carry the physical scar to this day.

My wife and I laugh over that story now, but deep inside I still remember how it felt to be awkward and embarrassed. Other tweenagers have those same feelings, and they need to hear words of affirmation, love and encouragement. I want them to have someone to look toward for support, friendship and emotional and spiritual leadership. That is why I am a junior high youth pastor.

Too many times I have met bitter, broken and confused students in senior high school who carry battle scars from junior high. Many are caught in a web of apathy, never having resolved those crucial questions of self-worth and identity. Men and women who work with senior highers often spend hours simply trying to salvage spirits broken in junior high school when they ought to be preparing teenagers for the threshold of adulthood.

When tweenage ministry is well done, it is an invisible investment, a firm foundation which cannot be shaken through the ensuing years.

The Toughest Job You'll Ever Love

We're the first to admit that tweens can be a difficult age group to work with. But *someone* has to be willing to risk some personal comfort. Tweenagers don't care how old you are or whose parent you are—they simply need someone who cares enough to be consistent.

What special qualities does it take to work with tweenagers? Patience, a lot of love, a sense of humor, honesty and the ability to never be (or act) shocked.

It is also important to be transparent with middle schoolers. If you have a hidden agenda or a subconscious reason for working with them, they'll discern it in no time. If you think taking your kid to a football game will get you a "Father of the Year" nomination, or if you're trying to win points with your pastor by volunteering in the youth department, no tweenager will take you seriously.

Middle schoolers aren't children any more. They've learned enough about the adult world to recognize hypocrisy, and they're blunt enough to point it out.

If you're making a token effort to be with tweenagers

- to impress another adult
- to ease a guilty conscience
- to fulfill a hastily-made promise
- to tag along with your spouse
- to keep an eye on your kid
- or to give an impression of being "young and crazy"

you've got the wrong motivation.

The only correct motivation for being with tweenagers is love. They only want—and desperately need—someone to love them through this crazy stage of adolescent development.

As you organize your life this week, think about the tweenager you love. How can you change your love into an action? By recognizing what is urgent and what is important:

Urgent things demand instant action.

Important things require careful attention.

Urgent things clamor loudly.

Important things are most often quiet and unobtrusive.

Urgent things are many.

Important things are few.

Urgent things are resolved and soon forgotten.

Important things, though eternal, are often neglected.

What is urgent? A report demanded by your boss; a meeting with big-name people; a reckless drive through traffic to catch a flight.

What is important? The time you spend with your family, laughing, loving and sharing; the time you spend with God and in prayer; the time you spend one-on-one with a tweenager who needs you.

Remind your tween that he is precious to you and to God.

Teach him that life is full of joys and sorrows, but that God always brings us through the difficult times stronger than we were before.

Respect his growing independence and allow a measure of privacy.

Instruct him by assessing fairly his requests for privileges and responsibilities.

Most important of all, love him by being there when he needs you . . . with an open ear and a receptive heart.

Recommended Reading

Hunt, Angela. *Loving Someone Else's Child.* Wheaton, IL: Tyndale House Publishers, 1992.

Hunt, Gary and Angela. *Now That He's Asked You Out* and *Now That You've Asked Her Out.* San Bernardino, CA: Here's Life Publishers, 1989.

Marshner, Connie. *Decent Exposure: How to Teach Your Children About Sex.* Brentwood, TN: Wolgemuth & Hyatt, 1988.

McDowell, Josh. *Why Wait?* San Bernardino, CA: Here's Life Publishers, 1987.

Penner, Clifford and Joyce. *A Gift for All Ages.* Waco, TX: Word Books, 1986.

Scott, Buddy. *Relief for Hurting Parents.* Nashville, TN: Oliver Nelson Publishers, 1989.

Veerman, David. *Reaching Kids Before High School: A Guide to Junior High Ministry.* Wheaton, IL: Victor Books, 1990.

Notes

Chapter One

1. Louise Ames, Frances Ilg, and Sidney Baker, "A Parent's Guide to the Tween Years," *Redbook* (June 1988), p. 148.
2. Thomas J. Cottle, "The Connections of Adolescence," *12 to 16: Early Adolescence* (New York: W. W. Norton & Company, 1972), p. 299.
3. Edward C. Martin, "The Early Adolescent in School," *12 to 16: Early Adolescence* (New York: W. W. Norton & Company, 1972), p. 181.
4. Martin, "The Early Adolescent," p. 182.

Chapter Two

1. Patricia Sherlock, "To Meg, on Becoming Thirteen," *Reader's Digest* (December 1987), pp. 189-90.
2. Jerome Kagan, "A Conception of Early Adolescence," *12 to 16: Early Adolescence* (New York: W. W. Norton & Company, 1972), p. 100.
3. Adapted from Bruce B. Barton, "Identity Crisis in Teenagers," *Parents and Teenagers* (Wheaton, IL: Victor Books, 1984), p. 158. Used by permission.
4. Personal interview with Clyde Narramore, April 28, 1986.

Chapter Three

1. James Dobson, "The Most Difficult Period of Adolescence," *Parents and Teenagers* (Wheaton, IL: Victor Books, 1984), p. 157.
2. James S. Coleman as quoted by Chad Gordon, "Social Characteristics," *12 to 16: Early Adolescence* (New York: W. W. Norton & Company, 1972), p. 39.
3. Edward C. Martin, "The Early Adolescent in School," *12 to 16: Early Adolescence* (New York: W. W. Norton & Company, 1972), p. 190.
4. Urie Bronfenbrenner, *The Ecology of Human Development* (Cambridge: Harvard University Press, 1979), p. 284.
5. Urie Bronfenbrenner as quoted by John Janeway Conger in "A World They Never Knew," *12 to 16: Early Adolescence* (New York: W. W. Norton & Company, 1972), p. 221.
6. Martin, "The Early Adolescent," p. 192.
7. John Janeway Conger, "A World They Never Knew," *12 to 16: Early Adolescence* (New York: W. W. Norton & Company, 1972), p. 221.

8. William Bennett, a speech given at Liberty University, Lynchburg, Virginia, April 23, 1986.

9. *Children and Parents: Together in the World,* Report of Forum 15, 1970 White House Conference on Children (Washington, D.C.: Superintendent of Documents, 1971).

10. Kathleen McCoy, "Help Your Child Beat Peer Pressure," *Reader's Digest* (May 1991), p. 68.

11. McCoy, "Help Your Child," p. 67.

Chapter Four

1. James Dobson, "Why Teens Don't Like to Be Seen with Their Parents," *Parents and Teenagers* (Wheaton, IL: Victor Books, 1984), p. 195.

2. Gregory Monaco, "Your Teen Wouldn't Swear, Would He?" *Parents and Teenagers* (Wheaton, IL: Victor Books, 1984), p. 190.

3. Lawrence Kohlberg and Carol Gilligan, "The Adolescent as a Philosopher," *12 to 16: Early Adolescence* (New York: W. W. Norton & Company, 1972), p. 153.

4. Personal interview with Surgeon General Koop, January 18, 1987.

5. "The Only Thing Wasted Is You" (Silver Spring, MD: National Federation of Parents for a Drug-Free Youth).

6. Adapted from "Hey Girls—Look What Alcohol Can Do For You" (Silver Spring, MD: National Federation of Parents for a Drug-Free Youth).

7. Felix Winternitz, "Look Out! Here Come the Tweens," *USA Weekend* (May 27-29, 1988), p. 4.

8. Winternitz, "Look Out!"

9. Winternitz, "Look Out!" p. 5.

Chapter Five

1. Louise Bates Ames, Frances Ilg, and Sidney Baker, "A Parent's Guide to the Tween Years," *Redbook* (June 1988), p. 150.

2. Thomas J. Cottle, "The Connections of Adolescence," *12 to 16: Early Adolescence* (New York: W. W. Norton & Company, 1972), p. 296.

3. Cottle, "The Connections of Adolescence," p. 296.

4. James Dobson, "Dr. Dobson Answers Your Questions," *Focus on the Family* (February 1989), p. 21.

Chapter Six

1. Grace Ketterman, M.D., "Positive Rebellion," *Parents and Teenagers* (Wheaton, IL: Victor Books, 1984), pp. 485-86.

2. Arthur L. Stitchcombe, *Rebellion in a High School* (Chicago: Quadrangle Books, 1964), referred to by David Bakan in "Adolescence in America," *12 to 16: Early Adolescence* (New York: W. W. Norton & Company, 1972), p. 84.

3. Adapted from James Dobson, *Dr. Dobson Answers Your Questions* (Wheaton, IL: Tyndale House, 1987), pp. 270-72.

4. Buddy Scott, *Relief for Hurting Parents* (Nashville, TN: Oliver Nelson Books, 1989), p. 10.

5. Nina Darnton, "Committed Youth," *Newsweek* (July 31, 1989), p. 66.

6. Personal interview with Buddy Scott, February 6, 1990.

7. Scott, *Relief*, pp. 187-88.

8. Personal interview with Buddy Scott, February 6, 1990.

Chapter Seven

1. James Dobson, "Your Teens are Growing Up Faster Than You Did," *Parents and Teenagers* (Wheaton, IL: Victor Books, 1984), p. 176.

2. Grace Ketterman, M.D., "Why Girls Mature Faster Than Boys," *Parents and Teenagers* (Wheaton, IL: Victor Books, 1984), p. 178.

3. Josh McDowell, *Why Wait?* (San Bernardino, CA: Here's Life Publishers, 1987), p. 79.

4. Personal interview with Connie Marshner, July 5, 1988.

5. Clifford and Joyce Penner, *A Gift for All Ages* (Waco, TX: Word Books, 1986), p. 105.

6. Personal interview with Surgeon General Koop, January 18, 1987.

7. Wayne Rice, "Challenging Media Myths About Sexuality," *Christian Parenting Today* (September/October 1989), pp. 79-80.

8. Personal interview with Connie Marshner, July 5, 1988.

9. Connie Marshner, *Decent Exposure* (Brentwood, TN: Wolgemuth & Hyatt, 1988), pp. 177-78.

10. Marshner, *Exposure*, p. 31.

11. McDowell, *Why Wait?* p. 79.

12. Personal interview with Norman Geisler, March 16, 1987.

13. J. M. Tanner, "Sequence, Tempo, and Individual Variation," *12 to 16: Early Adolescence* (New York: W. W. Norton & Company, 1972), p. 19.

14. Paul D. Meier, *Christian Child-Rearing and Personality Development* (Grand Rapids, MI: Baker Book House, 1977), p. 180.

Chapter Eight

1. Jerome Kagan, "A Conception of Early Adolescence," *12 to 16: Early Adolescence* (New York: W. W. Norton & Company, 1972), p. 93.

2. James Dobson, "Dr. Dobson Answers Your Questions," *Focus on the Family* (September 1989), p. 9.

Chapter Nine

1. Ron Hutchcraft as quoted by Dave Veerman, *Reaching Kids Before High School* (Wheaton, IL: Victor Books, 1990), p. 18.

2. Urie Brofenbrenner as quoted by John Janeway Conger, "A World They Never Knew," *12 to 16: Early Adolescence* (New York: W. W. Norton & Company, 1972), p. 199.

3. Personal interview with Norman Geisler, March 16, 1987.

4. Susan Tifft, "Help for At-Risk Kids," *Time* (June 26, 1989), p. 51.

5. William Bennett, a speech given at Liberty University, Lynchburg, Virginia, April 23, 1986.

6. Urie Brofenbrenner as quoted by William Bennett, a speech given at Liberty University, April 23, 1986.

7. For more information on stepparenting, see our book, *Loving Someone Else's Child* (Wheaton, IL: Tyndale House Publishers, 1992).

8. "Teen Suicide Rate Soars Even Higher," *Focus on the Family* (July 1986), p. 4.

9. "Teen Suicide Rate," p. 4.

10. Jeannye Thornton, "Behind a Surge in Suicides of Young People," *U.S. News and World Report* (June 20, 1983), p. 66.

11. Mary Ann O'Roark, "The Alarming Rise in Teenage Suicide," *McCall's* (January 1982), p. 16.

12. O'Roark, "The Alarming Rise," p. 22.

13. O'Roark, "The Alarming Rise," p. 120.

14. "What Predicts Adolescent Suicide?" *Essentials of Adolescence* (Volume 9, No. 4, 1983), p. 1.

Helping Your Kids
Through Adolescence